MARRIAGE WITHOUT PRETENDING

MARRIAGE WITHOUT PRETENDING

Anne J. Townsend

SCRIPTURE UNION
130 City Road, London EC1V 2NJ

© *Anne Townsend 1975*

First published 1975
Reprinted 1976, 1981, 1983
ISBN 0 85421 543 4

Printed and bound in Great Britain by
Purnell (Book Productions) Ltd, Paulton, Bristol.

Contents

Note from the Author

Some of my fellow-missionaries and friends are frightened that they will find themselves and their marriages appearing in print in this book! May I assure them, and all readers, that while all the descriptions of marriages in this book are based on fact, I have obtained this information from people who are not (as yet) personal friends of mine. Moreover, and to avoid identification, names have been changed.

I would especially like to thank 'Pam' and 'Liz' on your behalf for their costly honesty in sharing their problems with you.

Anne Townsend
OMF Christian Hospital,
Manorom,
Thailand.

1. Under the Mask

'Strangers that pass in the night' was the phrase passing through my mind as I gazed at her.

We eyed one another, both sensing that this was one of those very rare occasions in which one person was going to be able to share a deep problem which she had never revealed to anyone else before. I felt her courage and confidence growing, as she mentally pigeon-holed me as 'missionary from Thailand' and 'safe to confide in, because we'll never meet again'.

I sipped my hot tea, giving her the silence she needed to open her innermost heart to me. She absent-mindedly swirled her spoon around the teacup. Her drab twin-set was in the same uninteresting colour as her tea. Her lifeless, straight hair emphasized her angular nose. Her rough hands fiddled incessantly with her teaspoon, over a dull tweed skirt. I mentally labelled her as 'probably a very sensible and reliable person', and wondered whatever someone as 'respectable' as she was would want to share; it was obviously something costly for her to admit.

The hot tea, a warm fire, and a stranger prepared to listen gradually loosened her tongue. Her story came haltingly at first, but gradually the flow of words could not be quenched. Her outer mask of middle-class respectability was lowered slightly to reveal a vulnerable and hurt woman inside. It was obviously costly to her to lower this mask. The world usually saw only the outer mask of a successful wife and mother, who ran several local women's organizations and was a reliable member of her church.

Perhaps I was the first to be given a glimpse into the inner woman who, for years, had suffered silent misery, and become twisted and bitter inside because of her unhappy marriage. For many years she and her husband had failed to communicate with one another; they now slept

7

in different rooms. Because their youngest child had recently married, they were left with nothing in common, nothing which they could share.

Her eyes were deep and hopeless as she made the costly admission, 'The only reason we live in the same house is that we're afraid of the comments of people in the church if we live apart. . . . You see, they think we're the ideal older married couple . . . no one knows what it's really like. . . .'

She pulled herself together, and I could see she was raising her mask again. She was now determined to regain her glossy, successful exterior at all costs. She was virtually refusing even to face up to the fact that her marriage had gone wrong. She had no intention of trying to clear up the inner stagnant mess in her life. She had no idea how her husband viewed their marriage. They communicated about basic necessities only. Over the years, acceptance in their church group had become more important to her than daring to face honestly, and then attempt to sort out, her marriage. She was approaching late middle-age, and perhaps felt it was now too late and perhaps not even worth the effort of trying to remake a relationship with her husband.

She disappeared from my life, making me freshly aware and newly sensitive to the fact that problems existed in the marriages of some Christians. I had been vaguely conscious of this fact before, but taken little notice of it. I discovered that she was not unique, and that I was seeing only the tip of an iceberg. Marriage for a Christian was neither automatically nor necessarily the 'heaven on earth' depicted by some romantics. To my surprise, some facing deep problems were those Christians rated by others as 'the most spiritual'.

I was naïvely surprised to discover the truth behind the comment of a friend, 'I suspect that many evangelical Christians still believe that spirituality in a limited sense is the answer to all problems. They *cannot* believe that men who are marvellous in the pulpit, and on church committees, and who are looked up to for their spiritual

8

wisdom and maturity, can nevertheless be failures and even disasters to their wives.'

The truth of these words came home to me when I heard of one clergy couple. Beatrice, the busy, no-nonsense vicar's wife, puts on a brave front to the world. She gives herself completely to the parish, and tries to support her husband up to the hilt, in his work for God. A friend of hers sees under Beatrice's wan smile and comments, 'When they married, Jim was a new young clergyman. He was very autocratic, while she was sensitive and longing for close affection. He plunged wholeheartedly day and night into the pressing demands of the parish. When he dragged himself home at night, he was far too tired to make love to Beatrice with any real interest. The parish had drained his physical and emotional resources.'

Their friend's eyes softened, and moistened as the story was unfolded. 'One day Beatrice came to me and sat sobbing her heart out with the frustration of loving this man : he was a man deeply dedicated to God : but somehow trying to love others for Christ's sake, had swallowed him up. He could not spot the desperate need of the woman closest to him to be given more of that man's love. Others had drained his resources, and she felt he could not love her fully.'

She loved him, and tried loyally to become the type of vicar's wife she knew her husband wanted her to be.

'But,' her friend commented poignantly, 'her wan smile does not hide the deep frustration in her eyes as she looks at Jim. . . .'

A few weeks later Liz, a younger friend, wrote, 'By the time I was thirty I had lots of boy-friends, but enjoyed my work so much that whenever marriage was mentioned, I ran away. Then I fell idiotically in love with a tall, dark, brown-eyed man. The world became a fantastic place. He was of all men the most handsome, and the most magnificent. . . . Wonder of wonders, I found that *he* loved *me*. Whenever we met in our courting days we kissed and cuddled, and walked around in a rosy dream. I had a few whispered qualms . . . we never talked on a deep personal level, except to discuss the reality of

9

Jesus Christ. I accepted him as the 'strong, silent male type'. On our first Sunday meeting I warned him that I wanted to go to church : he was then not a member of any church. I began to pray for him, and to ask God not to let my emotions run away with me.

'All my doubts were swept away when he announced that he had become a Christian. I took this to be God's seal to me that this *was* my man. We waltzed off to the altar to take life-long vows just six months after our first meeting.'

A decade later, Liz confided that she felt her husband had been 'still-born' in his experience of Christian new birth. Marriage to him now seemed almost intolerable. However, she had made vows to God to stay with this man until they were separated by death. She now felt both committed and trapped.

Without looking for Christian marriages in trouble, I was now beginning to stumble into them in unexpected places. A young man spoke to me at a University Christian meeting, unknowingly revealing that he was heading for trouble. Sincerity, idealism, and dedication to God shone out of his face as he told me of his desire to follow his Lord. He felt that God was calling him to give up his good prospects in England, to go and work overseas in the Third World. It was then that I noticed the ring on the fourth finger of his left hand.

I raised my eyebrows, 'How does your wife feel about it?'

'Her?' He looked faintly puzzled, 'We don't really talk about that kind of thing. . . .'

I had to persist, 'How long have you been married?'

'Eighteen months.' He seemed as if he wanted to learn something from me. He was open and innocent.

'Can't you talk to her?'

He shook his head, 'No, we just don't seem to get through to one another.' His transparent face registered his longing to be able to share things that really mattered to him with his young wife.

People like these Christians were making me re-think my ideas about Christian marriage – ideas assimilated in student days, and never carefully thought out for myself before.

I heard of Harry and Joan who were committed Christians. They married in their mid-thirties. Before knowing one another, they had never made any close friendships. Their courtship was brief, and expression of love through touch was limited to the occasional peck of a kiss, and holding hands.

After they had married, Harry discovered to his dismay that Joan saw little place for sexual intercourse within marriage, apart from the purpose of conceiving children. She allowed him to 'use her' (an expression of hers which embarrassed him, and he hated) only when she wanted another baby. Once their family was complete, intercourse was completely excluded from their relationship.

Harry faced an intolerable situation. He was a Christian, who longed to express his love in marriage through sexual union with his wife. Yet, Joan refused to see this as part of a normal and natural marriage. Harry was torn in two trying to sort out how, as a Christian, he should react to this situation. He felt he was heading for a mental breakdown.

He threatened to leave Joan : when threats made no difference, he actually walked out : but, as a Christian, soon returned, to the old stalemate. Her attitude was unchanged. He even sought help through marriage counselling. This produced complete deadlock with the impasse of Joan indignantly declaring that help was quite unnecessary. She was right and he was wrong.

As I heard of them, I mused, 'Here's a fine Christian couple *outwardly* . . . but there's trouble *underneath*. Can their marriage possibly survive? How many more are there who like Harry want help and can't get it; and like Joan can't even see they need help?'

I discovered that I had blissfully and thoughtlessly assumed that any marriage between any two Christians *must have been* 'made in heaven', and therefore must be 'heaven on earth'. The *facts* I was finding in some marriages were proving my assumption to be false.

If I was seeing the tip of an iceberg, how much more was submerged under water?

And as a friend said to me, 'Quite apart from the Christian marriages which are in real trouble, I believe there are many more that have settled down to a level of mediocrity, which is far less than God intended. This I think is partly because (wedding services apart) very little teaching is given as to what the Bible really says about marriage. All you get is the frequent and often furious warning that no Christian should ever marry a non-Christian, but as to the Bible's positive teaching about human relationships, including relationships between husband and wife, our churches are for the most part strangely and sadly silent.'

As I listened, and questioned, I discovered that some other Christians – besides myself – *were* asking questions about marriage. Some were genuinely trying to discover God's pattern, as shown in the Bible, for us in the twentieth century.

The first and most basic question that some people were asking was, 'Why get married? What's the point in it? Why can't we just live together?'

Problems abounded that needed sorting out. Questions were being asked that needed serious consideration.

2. Why Marry?

'Why do we have to get married?' summarizes a caco-phony of voices echoing in my mind from a year's leave in England. Voices from students, friends, television, radio, and magazines. Even a student *missionary* weekend finished on the last evening as a kind of group impromptu 'marriage guidance session' – with the inescapable question 'Why?'

A popular song-writer voices a thought lying behind some questions, 'Did I marry just to live in a little box-house, set in a row of more boxes? Will I produce children, who will themselves buy boxes, reproduce, per-petuate, and escalate a life of conformity in a land soon to be swarming with box-like houses?'

I suppose he could be given a blunt answer, 'OK! You married to maintain middle-class morality; to be socially acceptable; to maintain the *status quo* – and to be quite frank, if this was the only reason, then perhaps you mar-ried to save yourself from having to think out good reasons for *not* marrying!'

Quickly and superficially, it may seem easier and more truthful to present a case *against* marriage rather than to argue the case *for* marriage.

What about the argument in favour of 'trial marriages', in which a couple live together before marriage, to see if they are sexually compatible?

Perhaps Alan and Violet would have been saved much misery had they gone in for a 'trial marriage', before com-mitting themselves fully to one another. They were both Christians who came from broken homes. Alan's mother was neurotically dominant, while Violet's father was openly promiscuous. After a very short engagement, the couple married in their mid-twenties. Once married, they discovered to their bewilderment that Alan was unable to consummate their marriage. Violet was not mature enough to understand how to help and encourage him. Instead she began to tease and taunt him for his seeming failure. She became occasionally violent, and finally walked out on him without a word, never to return. After their marriage was annulled, Alan blamed himself deeply. Violet could not see that she might in any way have been responsible. She would not accept the possibility that responsibility might lie with both sides.

'Surely,' it might be argued, 'this Christian couple would have been saved deep emotional suffering had they lived together before marriage, and discovered Alan's sexual hang-ups before committing themselves to one another for life?'

'Yes!' it could be answered, 'they might have been spared this special type of suffering; but because they were sincere Christians, they would have inevitably run into deeper and more hurtful spiritual problems by contravening what they knew to be God's command to them not to practise sexual intercourse outside marriage.'

I shall never forget the pretty agnostic blonde student who told me about her 'trial marriage'. 'We had good sex together,' she confided, 'and got married because we enjoyed one another this way, and wanted our whole life to be one long honeymoon. The trouble is that, now the novelty has worn off, we've discovered we have little real love for one another. . . . What we had was purely physical.'

Her friend broke in, 'I really don't see the point of you having got married at all! Why did you bother? Anyone can get contraceptives nowadays. Why didn't you just live together, and only think about getting married if you became pregnant by mistake, or on purpose?'

The blonde was looking wistful, and as if life had cheated her somewhere and some time, 'I *think* I wanted more than sex – I wanted to be committed to him for life. I wanted to belong to a man. Otherwise, we could have gone "way-out"; lived in a commune, shared child-raising, and even partners, if that was the scene there.'

The argument *against* marriage continues. Some television programmes depict marriage as disastrous, and particularly detrimental to a woman's interests.

The successful career woman is shown running her motel, or supervising her prison. I watch her, see her husband as a hazy figure who features vaguely in every third episode (possibly I watch too infrequently to judge fairly), and wonder, 'Well, *what* is the point in Meg and Fay being married? Since the Industrial Revolution, women like them have had ample opportunity to live independently from men. Men are not *needed* to earn the money to support them; they can support themselves, and no longer need marriage to safeguard their status in life.' Even the career woman working at the conveyor belt in the factory often prospers on her own.

Society now accepts the single career woman : her life may be spared complication, frustration, and conflicting loyalties, should she *choose* to remain single rather than to marry. Some might say she should be spared the 'encumbrance' of a husband ! Sex should be freely available for such a woman, provided there is no intention of raising a family (so others would assume without any need for further discussion). Even at this point, eyebrows may be raised; 'Why do you keep on mentioning children?' someone asks.

I try to sound convincing, 'Because those who are responsible for conceiving children, are also responsible for seeing that they grow up in a secure family with both a father and a mother figure.'

I can anticipate these raised eyebrows, moving upwards even nearer the hair-line, with the response, 'Obviously it's because you're a missionary in Thailand that you're so behind the times. . . .'

I've heard their reply so often that I could give it myself now, 'Pregnancy no longer means a girl *must* get married. To begin with, more people want to adopt babies than there are babies available. So by all means produce the odd unwanted baby for those who want them. That's a public service ! Then, if a mother decides to keep her baby herself, it is much easier for her nowadays than it used to be. Haven't you even heard the term we've coined while you've been "lost" in Thailand? We now

15

have "single-parent families", who are becoming increasingly socially acceptable; we have clubs to which "single-parents" can belong; and a few organizations trying to help them.'

I nod, as the inevitable conclusion is churned out like a piece of indoctrination, 'So, pregnancy is no longer a valid reason for marriage.' I could try quoting statistics to show that a very high percentage of children who have run into trouble with the courts or the police, come from broken homes, or single-parent families. However, since I know of no research which shows how many children from such unusual homes, have been 'successful', this line of statistical argument is not completely valid.

The argument against marriage progresses logically and illogically. Perhaps the most subtle is the unconscious effect that the mass media have on unsuspecting and unarmed 'box addicts' like myself. Without realizing it we may fall for the advertiser's message that this or that will transform our lives. However, the people who I see transformed on my T.V. screen are often the singles. They are depicted (to me) as the young, glamorous, beautiful, and free. The marrieds seem to be trapped in a confining net. The latter are interested in paint, polish, and porridge; the former in sunbathing, water-skiing, and gazing at sunsets. Unconsciously I develop the picture that the fulfilled people of today are *not* the marrieds. The married are the fools!

Having argued a case *against* marriage, I can easily turn to history, sociology and psychiatry to argue a strong case *for* marriage.

However, as a Christian, my concern is to live my life God's way. Therefore, I need more than anything else to find out what *God* has to say in the Bible about marriage. His teaching on marriage will guide me, as a Christian, in a way that no other teaching can.

3. *The Master Plan*

'What's marriage got to do with church anyway?', blearily asks the man being interviewed on the T.V., as he raises another pint to his lips, 'Of course it's nice for the women . . . they like a bit of a dress-up, bridesmaids, flowers, and the mums having a good cry. . . .' His thoughts trail away into space.

His comments focus my wandering thoughts on the words, 'The *Church* didn't invent marriage : it was instituted by *God* Himself.'

Why then are ordinary non-church-going people married in church? Perhaps because deeply in their culture they have absorbed the thoughts behind these words, without realizing it. If God created marriage, then it is natural for those who are being married to celebrate their union in his house, in church.

As we read the Bible, we find that marriage was not man-made. It was actually designed and planned by God.

Right back when God created the world, He set up what some theologians refer to as 'creation ordinances'. This is not just a bit of technical jargon; it summarizes a truth that God wants us to understand.

'Creation ordinances' were set up by God when He was making the world, and while man still lived in close fellowship with Him. For this reason, it is argued, these are lines along which God intends *all* mankind to live. Their fulfilment is vital to man's functioning to his fullest potential. Because they were set up before man was estranged from God, it is reasoned that they are applicable to all people, whether they follow God or not.

Marriage is one of God's 'creation ordinances' : it is not something invented by man to fulfil his social and psychological needs. All creation ordinances apply to the *whole* of God's creation and not only to Christians. They are applicable to everyone. Thus marriage is for all people, and not only for Christians.

Looking at the first man, Adam, in the Garden of Eden, I am initially inclined to assume that he had everything he could possibly need. Why ever was his idyllic existence complicated by introducing a female into his perfect world? Surely his life would have been more peaceful and less complicated, if he had never had to go through the painful process of learning to build a relationship with a woman?

There were no ecological problems facing him! He was living in a beautiful and unpolluted environment. He should have experienced complete job-satisfaction; finding in his work responsibility, reward, and full use of his intelligence. He had no experience of the boring monotony of many jobs on the factory floor; nor the senseless, useless feeling arising from some forms of uncreative repetitive work.

Adam's 'job description' included that of 'subduing all things under him'. He had not learnt modern man's method of twisting this command to allow him to exploit that which should be governed in mercy.

He was the master of all, and the slave of nothing. He did not know what it was like to be an insignificant cog in the wheel of a vast industrial complex; nor how it felt to know that a computer could determine whether or not he was in or out of a job.

In addition to the satisfying work-load which he carried, God had given him another precious gift. His was the almost unbelievable privilege of being allowed to share a perfect, unique, and unbroken relationship with the great, Almighty Creator God.

What a life!

What a God to have created such a life for mere man!

Yet, God was aware of a vacant area in the personality of the man whom He had created. This man, created in God's image, was beginning to reveal himself as a person capable of social contacts, and needing meaningful relationships. Yet, he had only God and the animals with whom to relate.

He wistfully gives each animal a name to fit its nature,

yet is unable to build relationships with them. Man, who was created with the capacity for deep relationships, finds himself alone and isolated. Because he is made in God's image, he can never fully live until he has someone to love, and for whom he can sacrifice. The nature of God (Who within Himself forms a relationship between three Persons) is incorporated into man, in man's capacity to relate.

God, with His foreknowledge, knew the disastrous effects of what He was going lovingly and sacrificially to do for this man, to make him a whole person. God knew that it would not be long before man would become estranged from Him : and yet He loved him enough to pay the price of allowing the perfection He had created to be marred by man.

As he looked at Adam in his idyllic setting, God did *not* pat himself on the back, with a congratulatory, 'What a good job I've done there !'

Instead, he was moved to concerned action to fill the empty spaces in the man's life.

He stated, what to us now seems obvious, 'It is not good for man that he should be alone.'

Here the Bible gives the very clear reason why God planned marriage as the normal pattern of life for men and women. Quite simply, it is because they need one another.

All arguments about remaining unmarried *deliberately* contravene God's stated *normal* purposes for men and women. Marriage is seen as God's norm. Of course, there are exceptions. Jesus Himself was one notable exception. If a Christian girl decides she will marry only a Christian man, then she may well find she has no available marriage partner, since some churches contain many more women than men, though estimations vary tremendously from church to church as to the relative numbers of men and women in our churches today. Others may be led by God to a situation which excludes them from marrying. As Jesus explains, 'There are eunuchs who have been so from birth, and there are eunuchs who have been made eunuchs by men, and there are eunuchs who have made themselves eunuchs for the sake of the Kingdom of Heaven. He who is able to receive this, let him receive it.' The last class of 'eunuch' includes all those who have sacrificed legitimate, natural desires for the sake of the Kingdom of Heaven.

However, God's norm for man was that he should marry. God understood man's deepest needs, and saw what was needed to complete and complement him to make His creation perfect. Therefore, He brought into being another person, who was man's partner and counterpart on his own level.

He did not create a second male to meet this need. A homosexual relationship was not part of God's creation plan for man. God gave him a similar, yet a different, being – a woman.

She was of *value for herself* alone at this point : no mention was yet made of her role which was later to bear children.

The Bible calls her a 'help-mate'. This can delightfully be translated in other ways as, 'a helper meet', 'one adapted to', 'one who perfectly complements', and 'a helper as opposite to him'. This woman was obviously designed to play a vital role in the life of man.

As Adam had named the animals after their natures, and was able to appreciate personality, so he was able to appreciate this new being who had come into his life. He joyfully recognized her as someone made after the same pattern as himself : and yet he saw her as a wholly new being in her own right.

I wonder if he literally jumped for joy as he shouted in happy recognition, 'Bone of my bone !', when he met her for the first time.

Others have tried to convey his sense of wonder and pleasure by their translations of Adam's reaction, '*This* now *at last* !', or 'Boredom of my boredom : loneliness of my loneliness : success of my success.'

What a gift God had given man !

The woman was created from man's side as a symbol that she was to be his companion. As his wife she was to have a uniquely intimate relationship with him. She was the one who had been perfectly created and adapted to meet his needs. She was to complete, not to argue with him. They were mutually complementary.

This was why the Bible says a man is to 'leave' his parents, and to 'cleave to' his wife. The Bible does not give man an excuse to abandon his *responsibility* to his parents, but does make clear that he is to 'let-go' of them in the sense of the deepest of human *relationships*. The deep unity that should exist between a man and his wife will be hindered unless both loosen former close ties with parents.

Until old relationships are severed, new cannot be fully established. A marriage will be hindered in its growth as long as one or both partners are still dependent on their parents. The man who cannot adjust from his mother to his wife, on every level, may find the growth of his marriage is stunted.

The Bible taught that after a couple left their parents they were to 'cleave to' one another. This meaningless, old-fashioned word takes on a modern relevant meaning when translated as in its original use, 'to weld : to adhere tightly : to grip : to be separation-proof.' It reminds me of the art restorer, who takes two halves of an antique, invaluable vase, and glues them together, so that nothing can separate the fragments.

In a nutshell, 'to cleave' means that a couple should be so tightly 'stuck together', that there could be no thought like that of some contemplating marriage today, 'Let's give it a try. Then, if it doesn't work, we'll both behave like mature adults, and sensibly agree to separate.'

Jesus refers to the close unity formed by marriage when He says, 'They are no longer two but one,' or in another translation, 'They are one flesh.' I believe that He is referring to more than we sometimes appreciate. Not only is He speaking of sexual union, but He is referring even more deeply to the real uniting of two people or personalities. We tend to split man into compartments – physical, intellectual, and emotional. Jesus usually speaks of man as a total being. In an ideal marriage the 'two' become 'one' at all levels of their relationship.

It would be convenient and comfortable to believe that a man and a woman who have been 'welded together' by God in marriage, are thereby automatically cushioned from all stresses and strains in their marriage relationship.

It would be easy thus to imagine God as a kind of fairy godmother waving a magic wand over a couple, to ensure that they always lived in a rosy never-never land of dreams – excluded from the harsh realities of building and maintaining human relationships. Such wishful thinking is neither true to life, nor to the teaching of the Bible.

God never promised Adam and Eve immunity from life's problems, in the first marriage ever attempted. As they faced upheavals, so we should not be surprised if our marriages also run into problems. Their marriage possibly weathered the heaviest storms through which any marriage has passed.

Having been joined together by God, they rebelled against him, and lost their idyllic home in the perfect environment of the Garden of Eden. They eked out an existence in hostile circumstances as a result of severed relationships between them and their Creator; leading to broken relationships between man and man, man and woman. Their children proved a source of extreme anxiety to them, one murdering his own brother.

This marriage which had been created by God to perfect man was proving in practice to be far from being a bed of roses. Man had, by his rebellion against God, messed up not only his relationship with his Creator, but also with his fellow human beings. He was now especially vulnerable to broken relationships in marriage, life's closest relationship. Marriage that was given to man to complete and perfect him, now had the *potential* of twisting and destroying him. With Christ's redemptive action on the Cross man was later to have the option of restored relationships with God, and the potential of harmony with his fellow men – but this was to occur later in the New Testament era.

God did not expect Adam and Eve to walk out on one another when life got tough, nor to seek the escapism of refusing to face reality. He wanted them to work through their problems together, even when, humanly speaking, these problems seemed completely beyond help, or even hope.

This biblical ideal picture of marriage may lead some of us, ordinary Christians, to sink into a murky sludge of introspective depression. We may readily (or be faced unwillingly to) admit that God's *ideal* is far from *reality* to us. We may glimpse what our marriages might be potentially. Yet, at times our frail humanity prevents us from daring to imagine, hope, pray, and even work towards building the kind of marriage relationship we wistfully sense God wants us to have.

If we are the sort of people who tend gloomily to wallow in our inadequacy, then these words may encourage us to lift our feet out of their accustomed rut : 'It takes three, not two to make a marriage.'

This is not referring to the extra person in an eternal triangle, but rather to our Eternal God. The God who created marriage is the one who alone knows how to make it function as He designed it. The Holy Spirit, living within Christians, is able to radically change us. As he tranforms us, so this extends to the realm of our relationships with other people. As we are made gradually more and more like Christ, so our marriages are matured, and moulded to be more as God designed them to be.

If we have a niggling sense of dissatisfaction already about our marriages, then we can take one of two lines of action. We can have an enjoyable wallow in misery and self-despair, if we want to. On the other hand we can come to God in complete inadequacy, and ask Him to do something to make our stagnant marriage flourish and grow.

After I had been married about eleven years, my husband and I had reached a plateau of mediocrity. Demands on energy, time, and lack of privacy, led me to feel I was trapped under a mound of smothering blankets, under which no chink of daylight penetrated. My husband reacted much more positively. Pacing up and down on the beach one holiday, his angry outburst aimed at God was complaining in effect, 'God! Why have you done this? Why is there so much to do that I haven't time for my wife any more? Why are you tearing me apart in my loyalties?' God heard *his* cry of desperation, and pulled *me* out from my self-pitying wallow, so that together we were able to work again at developing our relationship.

God does not usually usurp or override the free-will which he has given to men. If we insist on our own independence of him, then he will allow *us* to make a mess of our lives and of our marriages.

However, if we genuinely long for our marriages to be as the Master Designer planned, then he will couple our human efforts on to his power. He expects us as rational, social, intelligent beings to try our human best to make relationships grow : but he does not leave us alone to struggle to achieve this. His help is ours for the asking.

Marriage as depicted in the New Testament is very simply : one man, one woman, exclusively and always. This makes it clear that a couple is not fulfilling the Creator's purpose if they are having sexual intercourse outside marriage. They make mockery of God's plan.

Marriage as designed by God involves life-long union in faithful love, to the exclusion of anyone else on either side. Since it is a permanent exclusive commitment to someone of the opposite sex, 'gay marriages', 'group marriages', and 'trial marriages' cannot be called 'marriages' in the New Testament usage of the word.

Having basked in idealism, we must face the hard-hitting realism of daily life. Marriage has been called 'a foretaste of heaven, or an anticipation of hell'. Liz experienced both aspects. She shares with us what it meant for her, *in experience*, to remain true to her vows to life-long, exclusive commitment to one man, regardless of what happened :

'We were going shopping one Saturday afternoon six weeks after our marriage, in our new mini-van. I offered to guide my husband into a small parking space at the side of the road. Hopping on to the pavement I ran to the front of the car, then to the back, signalling furiously. In this process the van got a six-inch long scratch on one corner.

'To me this was a minor matter but to my husband it was obviously the end of the world. He told me off as being the most careless, thoughtless woman in the world. He shouted and yelled. I started to cry, and still he marched resolutely through the shops, throwing over his shoulder at me the most unpleasant remarks he could find. My apologies went unheeded.

' "Dear God," I prayed, "now what do I do?" I couldn't run back home as my sister was in the throes of getting engaged and the family had enough problems.

'My husband strode into a furniture shop and sat down in the middle of a sea of armchairs. I searched the whole floor, couldn't find him, thought he had left me, and started crying again. When I finally found him, he *still* did not make it up....

'By that evening I hated my husband, and felt I had made a dreadful mistake in marrying him. But, when I began to pray I was reminded that I had promised to love, obey, and cherish this man until we were parted by death.

'I tried to wriggle out of this, "I know," I prayed. "I promised this, God . . . but I didn't know what *he* was like then."

'The words came back. "Did you promise *Me* or not?"

'I had to reply, "Yes, I promised *You*."

' "Then you must keep your promise, but I will help you," came God's voice.

' "Please Lord, give me back my feelings of love for my husband," I begged.

'Love did not return immediately, but came over the next few weeks, during which time I carried out my promise of behaving as if I felt love for him.'

God has designed marriage as a life-long, exclusive commitment between a man and a woman. Neither the Church, nor psychiatrists, nor social workers, nor anthropologists can claim to have invented it. It was God's idea.

Within God's plan of marriage is a vital factor, not yet mentioned but which is essential if a marriage is to work. This vital factor is that of *love*. 'Love' – the word we hear so often and understand so little. What is it, and how does it fit into marriage?

4. It Makes the World Go Round

Of course she knew the words of the song, 'Love makes the world go round,' but they had a hollow ring to her. Pam's marriage had broken down. She and Mike had been living apart for a year, after five years together. They had entered marriage with relatively little idea of the big step they were taking. Now she was sharing what had happened, as she saw it.

'Please use my story,' she invited, straightening her attractive dress. 'If any good comes of it, I'll be pleased.'

As she tucked her delightful children into bed, I turned the pages of her wedding album. I saw a kaleidoscope of normal, happy wedding photos. The bride and her family came from a well-known evangelical church, and were surrounded by a crowd of Christian friends and relatives.

If the bride's family had more money than the groom's, then it would not matter because Mike was motivated to work to his fullest ability, to try and give Pam the kind of home her parents had provided. She loved him, and felt she did not mind how they lived, if only they were together.

It had taken nearly two years for the couple to save enough money to be able to get a home, and marry.

They had first met in the coffee-bar run in Pam's church. Mike had come over with a group from his church, and had spotted her, serving coffee. He quickly singled her out as the girl who interested him. He found it easy to get to know her through attending functions at her church.

He said that he had become a Christian through contact with an evangelist from a well-known evangelical Christian centre.

She grew up in a Christian family. She was the kind of child who first asked Jesus to be her Saviour when she was three years old, and then repeated this every time she was naughty. The sudden discovery in her teens that her infallible parents had been wrong about something, made her question the Christian faith she had absorbed through them. If her parents *could be* wrong about anything, then they could be wrong about Christianity. This jolt made her seek a faith that was *her own* and not inherited from her parents. It led her to a search, culminating in the wonderful discovery that Jesus *was* real, and God *was* alive. Her parents' faith became part of her own life.

As she began to think for herself, she found it hard to sort out which of her parents' attitudes, ideals, and standards she should adopt as her own, and which discard as belonging only to an older generation.

Mike had said, 'If you're going to be my girl, then can't you do something about your clothes?' when they began to go out together.

Pam's immediate reaction had been to think, 'My father won't approve of me in trousers; he calls it "women wearing men's apparel", and says that "women in trousers are unbiblical" !'

She realized clearly that to begin to be a person in her own right, she *must* choose her own style of dressing. This meant deliberately asserting independence. She had bought a pair of clinging trousers, and a couple of tight sweaters, to replace her chunky knits and baggy skirts. She was half aware that she had made herself more sexually attractive for Mike's sake. She also knew that she had done something her father would not be pleased about.

When she went away from home to study, she was terribly lonely. She found no one in her year with a similar Christian faith. The other girls all seemed to have boyfriends, and many were engaged or married. Mike's friendship became more valued and precious in this situation than it had been when she was still at home, surrounded by the warm love of her family.

Mike and Pam saw one another rarely. This gave each meeting a tremendous build-up, and a sense of anticlimax when it was over. At first they sometimes prayed and read the Bible together as they had been taught Christian friends 'should', but this gradually petered out. Physical attraction gradually played a larger and larger part in drawing them together. They went on holiday together with other friends, and were obviously 'serious' about one another. Their names were linked in the church circles.

Parental disapproval added fuel to the fire. Pam *knew* her parents disapproved of Mike, but frustratingly she did not know *why*. They never told her, and she never ventured to ask. Her parents had been proved wrong by her before. They could be (*must be*) wrong about Mike, because she had decided she was going to marry him. She 'felt' God wanted them to marry, but could give no clear reasons for this 'feeling' of God's guidance. This 'feeling' of hers was strong enough for her to convince a concerned circle that God had really guided her to the husband of His choice.

They were often alone together during their engagement. As they were saving money, they did not want to spend any going out together. Evenings were spent cuddling in the car, or in Mike's room. The deep sexual attraction between them gradually, over months, made it easy for Pam to forget her upbringing and to allow herself to be petted to a peak of desire.

Mike's insistent 'Come on, *everyone* does, especially if they are already engaged' was hard to resist. She longed for sexual union with the man she loved.

At first she held back, knowing that her parents and church certainly would not approve. However, she *had* proved that her parents were not infallible. Perhaps they were wrong in this too? If 'everyone did', then *why* should she be different?

Her half-hearted resistance was eventually overcome, and she found that, contrary to all she had heard, sexual intercourse before marriage was for her a joyful and fulfilling experience. The physical side of their relationship was so attractive, that in retrospect Pam realized she had known very little else about what Mike was really like. He was a satisfying lover. She was to find later

29

through suffering that he was *not* the man she would have chosen to father her children; nor did he appear to be able to cope with keeping a wife and children at the standard he felt he ought to. This was a great strain for him. After many crises and because her children seemed in danger of psychological damage, she finally walked out and left him.

Pam stated, after her marriage had collapsed, 'Love-making before marriage helped to blur my vision of Mike and me as marriage partners. *I knew us as lovers, but not as people who would have to get down to the serious business of working to make a marriage grow.*'

In retrospect, Pam could see that she had walked into marriage, knowing very little about real love. Liz, too, found that love in marriage was not what she had imagined, 'The nature of love is not just in the feelings. It is not just a lovey-dovey emotion, it is more *a matter of the will.*

'When I first married, we were soon able to get a semi-detached house. I must admit that the house, furniture, carpets, and curtains did not interest me – they were just somewhere to live and aids to living. Similarly, house-work, washing and cooking took a very second place in my priorities. My husband grew angry when I took no interest in the choice of colours for carpets and curtains; and I couldn't understand his deep involvement in the dreary, long choices he made.

'My interest lay in "witnessing to non-Christians". I had a lot to learn, and God chose marriage to teach me. I hadn't a clue about housework. The dust would pile up, and I'd only see it when it was pointed out. I'd never had to clean a house myself before.

'When my husband called me a filthy slut, I turned in prayer to my Heavenly Father, "Lord, did you hear what he called me? How dare he!" I wanted revenge.

'As I bleated on to God, He made me look at myself.

'"You know his words are true, don't you? That's why you're so angry," God seemed to be telling me.

'I saw I had a big lesson to learn. Having a home, I

must clean it for my husband. I had to face his criticism squarely even though it was painful.

'*I realized that part of loving involved my will.* It involved my doing things for my husband, even if I didn't particularly want to. I was reminded of Jesus' words, "He that hath my commandments, and keepeth them, he it is that loveth me." '

How many of us, like Pam and Liz, enter marriage, thinking we know all there is to know about love? It takes years for some of us to realize just what 'love' in all its different aspects, is all about. At least we can, in our ignorance, find comfort in the phrase, 'we learn to love by loving.'

A late evening stroll around Piccadilly Circus in London leaves no excuse for failing to realize one of the meanings of the word 'love'. The statue of Eros, the ancient Greek god of love, surrounded by pimps and prostitutes in shady corners or darkened cars, brings home the fact that 'love' is associated with fulfilling sexual needs. 'Love' and 'lust' may be confused in our language and thinking. The trade and commercialization of erotic love may lead to a Christian being repelled by all that is associated with it. How can he have anything to do with the squalor of sex shops, pornographic books and magazines, and blue movies? He cannot! He follows a Master who has taught him, 'Whatever is *pure*, whatever is *lovely*, whatever is *gracious ... think about* these things.'

Perversion and misuse of erotic love by others should not, however, lead the Christian to assume that sexual expression within marriage is anything other than one of those 'pure, lovely and gracious' matters, which the Bible recommends he should 'think about'. Reading the Song of Solomon emphasizes love's purity, loveliness, and graciousness. Fulfilment of sexual lust should *not* be confused with normal erotic love, which has a rightful place in marriage.

Peter and Julie fell into this trap, so that their marriage is now devoid of the sexual love which God intended them to enjoy. They have known one another for ten years. Before they married, they touched one another passionately once or twice, as many engaged couples do. However, this led them to experience a deep sense of shame. They were ashamed that as Christians they had experienced some degree of sexual desire. The thought of intercourse now disgusts them; neither dare approach the other for fear of being spurned, and throughout their years of marriage they have never known sexual union. They are described as 'salted away and both prematurely crabbed and ageing'.

Erotic love should play a significant place in Christian marriage : the pure love and passion of physical attraction.

Equally important is the kind of love which C. S. Lewis calls 'Gift love as opposed to Need love'.

This kind of giving love (or *Agape*) was first made really clear to us in the quality of love Jesus had for humanity; it is the selfless love Christians are supposed to show in their dealings with one another.

I am human, and am terribly and basically selfish. 'I want . . . I don't mind what you need!' so often governs my actions, and my relationship with my husband. As I see it, the only hope for me is to *want* to be able to give my husband this selfless 'gift love' or *agape*. If my *will* is determined to try and attain this, then God can begin to pour this love, of which He alone is the source, into my selfish cold heart.

As a married couple actively want to develop the type of love that gives, so they will find that God is able to give this love to them. Love built on emotions is at the mercy of moods, weather, 'flu bugs and so on. A stable love, which is not influenced by inner or outer circumstances, arises from an attitude of *will*.

True love within marriage usually involves both erotic and *agape* types of love. All this love goes to make part of a total caring relationship. It is the formation and fostering of this relationship that is fundamentally what marriage is all about.

Two people come together in love. They then have a long, sometimes hard road along which to travel, in order to develop their relationship. Christians seem notoriously bad at taking the development of this relationship seriously.

Some glibly and naïvely assume, 'We are one in Jesus, therefore everything must be all right!' They wear blinkers over their eyes to hide from themselves the fact that theirs is a static relationship. They go through the accepted formulae for Christian marriages, but perhaps fail to hear Jesus' words, 'You whitewashed sepulchres!' The tragedy is that they have even failed to see that they are missing anything.

Others have a vision of their marriage as they believe God wants it to be. However, loyalties become a tangle of conflicts about the use of time and energy, and it seems that the simplest way to resolve them is always to put church activities before wife and family.

'After all,' it may be argued, 'Jesus said we were to "hate our husbands, wives and children" for his sake. Of course we put God and his interests first in our lives.'

I wonder if Jesus ever looks at the husband of an 'evangelical widow' and wants to gently and sympathetically rebuke him, 'My son, I love you and your love for Me . . . but you've got yourself muddled up somewhere. Sitting on all those committees and accepting so many preaching engagements isn't always the same as putting Me first in your life – especially as your relationship with your wife is pretty shaky and you haven't even noticed her much for a long time. . . . I, the Lord of love, have never asked you to starve your marriage of love, have I?'

Perhaps such a man, with shame in eyes, and perplexity of heart at his conflicting loyalties is able to confess, 'Lord, I've been terribly wrong . . . and I feel even worse since, as you know, I've done it partly to maintain a good front at church and never be accused of "losing out spiritually".'

Neglect cannot lead to the healthy growth of marriage relationships which God intends us to experience.

Of course there are the exceptional circumstances in which a couple cannot be together. A well-known Christian leader says, 'The enjoyment of the fact of union should only be forgone in a real situation of pressure or emergency, in which the Lord and His kingdom simply must have precedence. Then, and then only, is it legitimate, even necessary, for a man to put Christ before wife. If such "separation" is unavoidable, then I don't believe a marriage will actually suffer if (a) you simply cannot avoid this kind of "separation" (due to external pressures) (b) you humbly accept it together from the Lord without resentment, and (c) you trust each other.'

Love may 'make the world go round'. The song makes it sound so easy. Yet we discover that we have to learn to love; and learning to love takes time and effort. Personally, I feel it is a small price to pay for the invaluable gem of a growing relationship with another person. I'm speaking the truth – not merely a pious cliché for a Christian book!

5. *Loving is Giving*

'Of course I love my husband,' I mentally congratulate myself. 'Why, I'd sacrifice anything in his interests.' I smile smugly as I imagine the sweeping gestures of generosity which my fantasy world creates. He becomes paralysed or blind, and I become his heroic wife overnight, in my imagination.

However, learning to love is carried out in the real world of everyday petty affairs for most of us. For Liz, the depth of her love was tested in whether or not she remembered to turn off an electric switch : a seemingly trivial matter, but one of vital importance in her developing relationship with her husband.

She says, 'In early marriage I'd cook something, take it out of the oven and serve it. After the meal my husband always passed the cooker, where the switch had, as usual, been left on.

' "How many times have I asked you to turn it off immediately you've finished!" he would thunder. "It's such a waste of electricity. . . ."

' "I can't remember . . ." I tried to be bold.

'Finally, one day my husband could bear it no longer and shouted, "If you love me as you claim to, then why don't you *do* the things I ask you to ?"

'His words hit home : my memory is almost phenomenal now.'

The loving which is 'gift love' does not usually take place in front of captive audiences, T.V. cameras, and applause of men. It is usually that hidden giving which mentally says, 'OK, I squeeze the toothpaste in the middle and it drives you crazy . . . but because I love you, I'll try and do it from the end in future,' or 'I hate to see a room in a muddle, but because you can't bear a home to look like an hotel room, for your sake, I'll learn not to complain about the odd things left lying about,' or

35

'There's no reason why we should always watch *my* favourite T.V. programmes and listen to *my* choice of music!'

The wife who has been cooped up in the house all week and wants to go out at the week-end, may express her love by staying in because she knows her husband longs for nothing more than the peace of his home, and shelter from life outside. On the other hand, such a husband may express his love, by offering to take her out, when he most desires a roaring fire, a deep armchair, and a day dozing with the newspaper on his knee.

As a couple grow to truly love one another, they soon discover that mutual self-giving is an essential ingredient in their growing relationship. Our selfish human nature all too often creeps in and stifles growth. We are so blinded that we often fail to realize what is happening.

A wife may feel she is totally unselfish as far as her husband is concerned. She may be trying genuinely to do everything she can to help him. Yet this attitude may be coupled with a deep sense of possessiveness.

'I give him everything,' she may try to explain to a friend, 'yet he *still* wants to hang on to some of those friends of his.' She is exasperated, and cannot understand.

'Why shouldn't he?' the friend wonders.

'Well,' the wife admits, 'I can't understand what they're talking about when they get together. I feel shut out and excluded while they go on and on all night. . . .' Her mild regret that she is not more clever comes out in her tone of voice.

Dare the friends speak the truth? 'Although you love one another deeply, *you* can't and never will satisfy each other in *all* areas of your lives. Isn't it reasonable for him to seek the mental stimulation and intellectual growth these friends give him? Could it be a small area of selfishness which makes you resent these friends?'

A husband too may find, deep within himself, a possessive selfishness which leads him to try to suppress his wife's creative potential. He does not like the thought that she might need something, or someone outside himself.

Therefore he stifles her desires, and prevents her personality from maturing fully.

The subtleness of petty selfishness may mar many marriages, and stunt the growth of mature relationships.

Due to a quirk in human nature, some of us delight in swinging from one extreme to the other. The love that gives led Pam to adopt an extreme view. She had to ask herself whether real loving meant that a Christian should be a 'door-mat' over which his partner tramples at will? Pam was told, after her marriage had broken up, that in her relationship with Mike she had been too passive.

As he did not like classical music, this was never played while he was in the house. As he did not offer to help with the housework or children, she did not ask him to. He was used to breakfast in bed, and would complain if Pam forgot to *stir* the sugar into his coffee!

She gradually found she was rebelling against this. Surely he could manage to stir the coffee she carried to him? Surely, she reasoned, he should be weaned from such attitudes now he was an adult?

In the best interests of the other partner, a 'door-mat' type of self-sacrificing is not what God wants. Neither the childishly spoilt husband, nor the fussy, petted wife has developed to full maturity; and their growth may have been *hindered* by their partner.

Many of us find that learning to love is harder than we had expected. Self-sacrifice must go hand in hand with the common sense which sees whether or not certain sacrifices are in the best interests of the other partner. We discover that marriage is not so much a case of finding the right partner, as of being the right person. The love which seeks to give, rather than get, may at times be costly to us.

It would be easy for many of us Christians to feel that we should never quarrel or be angry in our marriages. We've all heard glowing reports of the 'perfect couple who have never argued throughout their fifty years of wedded bliss'. We've all heard the whispered condemnation, 'Fancy, the vicar's wife actually slammed the door in his face. . . .'

We may have adopted an axiom, 'To be Christian, and

to be married, is never to express deep unconventional and unexpected feelings to your partner.'

What happens to the normal couple, who *do* feel deeply and differently at times? For the sake of peace is one to play the role of hypocrite, and wear the mask of agreement? What happens to the fermentation under the mask? Will the unseen fermenting process explode one day like the cork that suddenly blows out of granny's ginger beer bottles in the cellar? Outwardly all is joy and light, until the explosion shatters and destroys. The ugly truth is suddenly seen under the veneer of light and peace.

I would challenge the assumption made by some that Christian couples should never disagree (granted there are times and places which are obviously unsuitable : and here the stability and security of children within the family must be considered). Why should a minister not be overheard having a row with his wife? He is then seen as normal, and therefore more approachable because he is human like everyone else. He no longer gives the impression of being an inhibited, shut-down man, who does not feel as the rest of the world does. Is our assumption that Christians should not be angry, carried out in play-acting before the world : living a lie : or wearing a mask? Jesus, the Truth, condemned hypocrisy. Jesus was not inhibited about his anger, when he drove money-lenders and cheats out of the Temple. His anger was just, selfless, and creative.

Of course there is a balance to be found in this. I am not saying that all vicars should chase their wives down the street with rolling pins! Somewhere, a couple need to find the middle path, in which they can express negative feelings, in the way that is natural for their personalities, without going to the extreme of always being at loggerheads. (Physical violence is normally unacceptable in our Western culture.) This varies with the couple's temperaments, upbringing and trust of one another. A good shout, a hefty slam of the door, or even smashing the loathed vase Aunt Aggie gave as a wedding present, may be turned creatively to deepen and develop a relationship.

A sense of humour may turn a potentially delicate situation into one that can be ultimately helpful.

My husband and I are not normally the 'rowing-types'. If, however, something sparks us off, we get going, reach a stalemate where neither will say 'sorry'; then the humour of a certain record can be guaranteed to have us so laughing at ourselves that we forget all the pent-up emotions we have just released. If one of us remembers to play the record of Peanuts 'I hate cats . . . I loathe them . . . they are the scum of humanity . . .!', within a few minutes we are in one another's arms, laughing, and secure in our love and deepened understanding of one another. Our ability to 'blow-our-tops', in the right place, and on the right occasion, has enriched our marriage. We have come to a deeper understanding of ourselves and one another through these times.

Real love imparts a sense of belonging to one another. Elderly, dear friends of ours have been married for forty years. As I look at them, I constantly marvel that after all this time they still find in one another a source of joy.

'Always remember to give your wife a cuddle and a kiss before getting up in the morning,' was the advice given to my husband by this husband, based on his long experience of years of loving his wife.

The pain in that husband's eyes, as he spoke recently of his wife's illness, and their separation at that time, was an unspoken tribute to their love and joy in belonging with and to one another. Separation had become painful for them.

The sense of belonging, that comes with loving, should make it natural for a couple to share everything with one another. However, after the initial glow of early marriage has worn off, a couple may need to work hard at sharing with one another. A breakdown in communication may occur imperceptibly and unintentionally.

Some men are so tired with 'work' that they come home and want to forget all about it. The husband may have 'home' and 'work' in different water-tight compartments in his mind. He arrives home exhausted, wants to forget the day, and escape into the newspaper or television. It may not occur to him to share the day's events and problems with his wife, nor that she might be hurt that he does not. He may not realize that such sharing (if his wife is able to keep his confidences) can be a source of tremendous strength to him.

Failure to share may be more deliberate. One partner may need the deep reassurance that sharing will not bring rejection. Unless there is confidence of acceptance, even in failure, sharing may be impossible for some people. Marriage, in the Bible, is used to illustrate the relationship between Christ and the Church. As the Church is forgiven and accepted with all its faults and failures, so in marriage should each partner find loving acceptance.

Admissions like, 'I made a stupid mistake today . . . I've a sinking feeling it will hinder my promotion . . .' or 'I just hated him for what he'd done to me . . . I almost wish him dead!' can either be received with the censorious attitude, 'You've let God and me down again, haven't you,' or with the love that seeks renewal and assures acceptance.

Some of us may fail to share because we want to live up to our partner's romantic, idealistic view of what we are. We do not feel accepted for the people we are, but rather for the people our partners imagine and desire us to be. Therefore we are afraid to expose our real selves. We need to discuss this frankly with our marriage partner.

Victor and Jean had not learnt to accept one another as they were (instead of what they would like one another to be). Their marriage ran into deep trouble. Jean was an insensitive girl, and although their sexual relationship in marriage was mutually satisfying, their mental and spiritual development was widely different. Jean could not express affection (although she claimed to feel it). Victor became irritable and emotionally withdrawn : he said he experienced only deep pain when he shared his emotional feelings with her, as she seemed to have no empathy or to understand his feelings. He then met another girl, also a Christian, and they had a long affair which was primarily a sharing of their emotional longings and frustrations . . . he sees little real future for any improvement in his relationships with his wife, and no long-term possibilities with his girl-friend. For years he has been burying himself in his work, as a substitute.

The ability to open one's deepest thoughts to another does not come instantaneously with the exchange of wedding rings. For some it may involve determined, costly effort, and risk of rejection. For others of us it may involve taking a long, hard, honest look at ourselves, and seeing how ugly we are inside. For many it takes years of hard work. Within the security of belonging, in a loving marriage, we embark on a voyage – calm where we agree; rough where we disagree; stormy as we re-think our positions, if we cannot reach the calm of agreement; and sometimes sailing the choppy waters of having to agree to disagree. Within such a framework of belonging, we can gradually become more closely united, even if we do not agree about everything.

'I don't need time to share! I know all there is to know about her,' leads some into trouble. We forget that, as individuals, each marriage partner may develop at different rates and grow in different directions. The man I fell in love with eighteen years ago, is not the man I love today. The man whose love I cherish today, has had to love a woman who has, over the years, changed imperceptibly. Yet, at each stage, he has somehow fallen in love with the new woman I have become. Love cannot be static because we are always changing; we need to love our partner as our partner is at each stage of life.

As a Christian couple grow in their relationship they learn how to give, and how to receive forgiveness, not only from God, but from one another.

Liz found forgiveness easy in theory, but difficult in practice :

'Quite often my husband would be very rude, and then refuse to speak to me for several days. I would try to remonstrate with him. It was almost unbearable to be living with someone, whom I loved, who would not speak to me : even when I begged him to.

'I would assure him I had already forgiven him, but

he said he could not accept my forgiveness because he had been too awful.

'God has used this agonizing situation to teach me wonderful lessons. Through this I can feel (in a small measure, at least) how God must feel; He loves all people, and yet the majority will not accept His forgiveness. God, the Forgiver, suffers . . .'

We may find it hard to forgive our marriage partner, and like Liz's husband may find it even harder to forgive ourselves for the things we have said or done. If Christ's sacrifice on the Cross forgives all sins, then it does not exclude the sins in our marriages. In accepting His forgiveness, we must learn to accept ourselves. God no longer blames us – does He tell us to continue blaming ourselves?

God does not tell us to blame our marriage partner and constantly nag and criticize. Thoughtless, or deliberate, criticism or sarcasm, or constant little comments underlining failures and weaknesses, do not enrich a marriage. Hand-in-hand with forgiveness, and acceptance of a person as he is, go the help and encouragement of positive praise of strong points and appreciation when an effort is made.

The Christian couple who are able freely to share their day-to-day spiritual experiences may be handling treasure so precious that they fail to realize its worth. There are few who are able to share that part of themselves which is the most intimate (that of their daily experience of the living God in their lives). They are frightened that what is a diamond to them, may turn to glass when seen through the eyes of another. A deep level of understanding and trust are necessary before sharing this part of ourselves with another person. Opening up the channels of communication may bring a breath of fresh life to a marriage which is growing stale. This may require effort, since many of us, because of our temperament and upbringing, are reticent about sharing anything other than the superficial. The mental and spiritual side of God's purpose that a married couple should be 'one flesh' will never be fulfilled if a couple fails to communicate.

Sexual intercourse then becomes the natural expression of true love between husband and wife. It should be symptomatic of complete sharing and companionship in every other aspect of life. Obviously neither can completely satisfy the other in all areas of life (e.g. intellectual stimulation; creativity : sensitivity and awareness of the same beauty; and pleasure in the same music). However, they are fundamentally complete in each other, and express their unity in the sexual bond.

Sexual intercourse thus becomes an act which is mingled with sacredness, as well as physical pleasure. Those newly in love often utter in wonder, 'But he's far too good for me . . . the whole thing is so beautiful and marvellous it can't be happening to *me*.'

As a Christian enters such a relationship of true love, he usually feels a deep sense of sacredness. His joy is intertwined with a thread of holiness. Such a deep sense of sacredness makes him reluctant (despite strong, normal physical urges) to mar God's gift to him by practising sexual intercourse before, or outside, marriage.

True love should make the Christian more and more like the Lord Jesus Christ. Not only are rough corners rubbed off in marriage, but the effort of will involved in sacrificial self-giving will make each partner more Christlike. A process the scholarly like to call sanctification.

So far, the sexual side of marriage has been mentioned only briefly. Does this mean it is unimportant? Is it only a necessary evil which deeply spiritual Christians should try and avoid?

6. Puritan or Playboy?

He was the prototype of 'attractive male' as he stepped waving and smiling from his personal black jetplane, with its Bunny Playboy symbols, gleaming with their stark whiteness on the sides of the aircraft.

He came into my sitting-room, at my invitation. I allowed him into the privacy of my home when I did not switch the television set to a different channel. Hugh Heffner, of *Playboy*, was saying to me winningly and smilingly, 'My aim is to try and bring some fun and pleasure back into our lives. . . .'

I nodded at the T.V. set, idly thinking 'Fine! What's wrong with pleasure! Surely, the God who created us with the capacity to enjoy life, does not intend us to live like shrivelled-up, dried prunes?'

The voice on the T.V. continued to expound the *Playboy* philosophy, and I realized that if I wasn't careful I was going thoughtlessly to accept teaching that as a Christian I could not accept.

I almost spoke aloud to the T.V. set : 'Of course there's nothing wrong with pleasure. *But* the Christian must be very careful here not to get his priorities scrambled – I am here in this world primarily to glorify God – to please him. The extent to which I find pleasure in the life God has given me to live, will be qualified by the extent to which the things I do please God . . . God is no kill-joy!'

I remembered a report in a Bangkok newspaper in 1973, which said that 'The United States is in the midst of a vast, profound and unprecedented sexual liberation movement, according to a survey published in *Playboy* magazine.

'The survey said that premarital sex has become both acceptable and widespread, with the change most noteworthy in women.

'The social changes related to sexual liberation have

44

been vast, profound, and unprecedented. Americans are more tolerant of the sexual ideas and acts of other persons than formerly; and far, far freer to envisage previously forbidden acts as possible for themselves. . . .'

No mention is made of some of the side effects that this 'sexual liberation' movement have had. Increasing incidence of divorce, abortion, and venereal disease are notable.

On a deeper level, the value of women has decreased. A woman is dehumanized when attached to the *Playboy* 'Bunny Symbol'. She ceases to become a person of value, and becomes a status symbol in the eyes of *some* men. In a world full of disposable items, she too can be discarded when she has served her purpose. At no cost must such a man allow her to 'get serious', or he will make the stupid mistake of marrying her. Sexual intercourse has been drastically devalued along with the dollar and the pound.

Some men in the twentieth century, while leading what they call a 'new sexual liberation movement', have given women little more status than that given by the legendary Puritan husband. He brought his wife to the City Fathers for trial, with the accusation, 'I am convinced that last night during intercourse I distinctly saw her smile.'

I switched off the T.V. quickly. This man with his teaching was no longer a welcome visitor in my house. I was, however, glad to have met him because he forced me to *think*.

Today, most Christian couples enter marriage with a brain well stocked with information about sexual intercourse. They have a clearer theoretical knowledge than their grandparents, and have clearly been taught 'the facts of life' and 'the birds and bees' by *someone* – if not by a loving adult, then from crude drawings on the wall in the school playground. The Christian couple are not so much lacking in knowledge of the physical act of union, as lacking in knowledge as to the meaning sexual union has for them. Their hang-ups may result from their deficient knowledge.

Liz found herself on her honeymoon, forced to try and

sort out in a crisis, rather than a calm situation, just what sexual intercourse was to mean to her. She bravely shares the truth.

'Every girl dreams of her honeymoon. Mine would be unblemished by previous furtive experience. I dreamed that all would be ideal – that I would be wafted to idyllic realms. I thought my husband would not be able to wait, that I was so desirable that as soon as we reached our hotel . . . but no. He launched into a long lecture about our not being animals but lovers only, and I felt scorned and unwanted. When I attempted to get into bed in the skin I was born with, I was rudely and coldly asked if I didn't normally sleep in a nightdress.

'Whom had I married? I came to a stunning discovery that I didn't really know him. If only we could have shared all our thoughts with each other, I would have discovered then how terrified he was of being unable to make love – the thought never entered my head.

'Early the next morning I was kissed awake, ordered not to move, used, and turned away from.

'Dear God, I prayed, what have I done? Here I am lying in bed with a stranger. How is it he has changed so much? I thought we'd spend the rest of our lives really understanding one another, growing to know you better, and serving you in our home together. Yet you saw how cross he was when I took my Bible to read it, and knelt to talk to you. Dear Lord, was *that* little exercise what they call making love? Is *that* what you meant it to be?'

'Much later we *were* able to talk about our "playing games". My husband invented the term. I think it helped us both to overcome our deep-rooted shame connected with sex. We found, after all, that it *was* a physical joy for us both. We were able to share with one another what we enjoyed best, where, how, and in what order each tried to please the other. 'Games' can be played any-where – what's wrong with the soft rug in front of the fire, as long as the children are asleep? Surely no one position is more 'worthy' than any other? Does it matter what, if anything, is worn?'

If we are honest, we have to admit that some, like Liz,

have found it hard to understand what sexual union is all about. We cannot accept the coldness and rigidity of Puritan teachings as we see them; nor the teaching of the New Morality which put in a nutshell (that does injustice to the teaching) says 'You can do what you like, as long as your motive is *love* and no one gets hurt'; nor the philosophy arising out of *Playboy* writers. Contemporary secular society does not help us.

Should we then, as Christians, not accept the teaching of the 'Christian world'?

I nod naïvely. 'Yes,' I think. 'That's the best thing to do. I should have done that first!'

I then pick up a very popular Christian magazine to discover that the evangelical Christian world is divided, muddled, prejudiced, and churning out clichés in its correspondence column as sexual intercourse is being discussed. A few letters shine with thought, and contemporary, honest, spiritual realism. The 'Christian world' is re-thinking its attitudes to sexuality – and, as yet, does not speak with a unanimous voice.

I shrug, putting away the magazine. It is back to the beginning, where I should have started in the first place. Of course, I knew that the Bible (God's Word to me) *must* be the basis for my behaviour as a Christian. However, seeking an easy short-cut, I had strayed away off my path, by trying to find answers in contemporary secular or Christian society.

It is back to the beginning to find out what *the Bible* has to say!

To listen to some people talking is to gain the impression that God and sexual intercourse cannot remotely be connected to one another. Nothing could be further from the truth. God was the Inventor of sex. Man, while talking as if he were its inventor, can only claim to have perverted one of God's most precious gifts.

God created sexual union, to be a normal part of marriage – man has perverted and misused it outside marriage and as God never intended.

God created the bodies of men and women, and designed their nervous systems so that sexual intercourse

47

would give them one of the most enjoyable and satisfying experiences of their lives. *He* made certain areas of the body responsive to sexual stimulation, and *He* made people aware of deep pleasure in such stimulation. *God* wanted them to appreciate to the full this tremendous bonus He had given. *He* wanted them to have fun, and enjoy this aspect of life within marriage.

Why then, in some marriages, is sexual union a furtive, almost shameful act; to be practised only in the dark under the bedclothes, and preferably as infrequently as possible? Is this glorifying the God Who designed mankind to glorify Him?

Some of us may have inherited hang-ups from our parents, making us guilty about sex, like Diana. She came from a broken home, and her mother had expressed her disillusionment with sex so strongly that Diana felt repelled emotionally by Martin, whom she loved and had married. She intellectually wanted sexual union with Martin, but never found the satisfaction she glimpsed could be hers. Her counsellor traces this back to her mother's attitude.

God intends us to find fulfilment, joy, and satisfaction in sexual intercourse. This rarely occurs overnight. Many newly-weds experience little pleasure in sexual union – they are shy, fumbling, frightened, and still learning. Within the security of love and commitment that marriage gives, a couple can learn together how to satisfy one another sexually : how to use different techniques to enhance the other's pleasure : they discover that a man's quick arousal is not usually speedily followed by the woman – he has to learn how to give her the extra time she needs before she is completely ready to culminate love-making.

Basic facts like these need to be learnt. The Christian is not exempt from the need to learn in this field, any more than he is exempt from going to school as a child, because he is a Christian. Knowledge of Jesus Christ does *not* give the key to automatic, instant happy sexual relationship, any more than it guarantees success in school examinations. There should therefore be no feeling of shame or failure, if a Christian admits his need to learn sexually and seeks knowledge from more experienced people, or written material.

His pleasure will be limited if he senses he is stepping outside the bounds of what *he* feels to be glorifying to God. Here individual Christian consciences differ greatly.

It is easy to use sexual intercourse as a means of expressing displeasure, or pleasure, at the behaviour of one's marriage partner.

'I'm not going to let him tonight, because he hasn't bothered to put up the shelves I wanted,' is not in line with the spirit of the Bible teaching, 'Do not refuse one another except perhaps by agreement for a season, that you may devote yourselves to prayer; but then come together again. . . .' God did not design sexual pleasure so that husbands and wives could use it to 'reward' or to 'punish' one another.

Sexual union was intended to be an act through which a married couple could joyfully and unashamedly indicate their deep union at many levels of life. In the context of a total relationship it is an expression of love. If the wife is 'used' as a 'body' by her husband, she may feel she is not a person to him but merely the object through which he satisfies his sexual urges. Such a union is not that which God planned it to be. No Christian should ever treat another person as a 'thing' and fail to respect his humanity. A husband who has a stronger sexual drive than his wife, may need to work hard to keep his wife with him, to make intercourse *fun* for her. It will then be a rewarding and worth-while experience for him, instead of sexual gratification only. He may need to use considerable patience and imagination.

Such effort was worth while for Pat and Angela. They were in their mid-twenties, and Christian youth leaders. For the first year of marriage, Angela put up with a basic kind of intercourse which was brief, and for her, unsatisfactory. She was never sexually fulfilled, and intercourse left her tense and keyed-up. They sought counselling, and revealed their mutual ignorance.

They left saying they would try again. After three

months Angela returned, and told their counsellor that Pat had hardly even attempted to put into practice the practical advice he had received. The counsellor arranged to see Pat, and told him pretty bluntly that he was not only irresponsible but that he was acting in an un-Christian manner for a husband. Pat was obviously annoyed, but agreed to make a real effort. A few weeks later, a glowing Angela met their counsellor. Pat's efforts had borne fruit! A normal, satisfying sexual relationship developed from that time onwards. Time and effort had been needed in this marriage.

God intends sexual intercourse within marriage to be joyful and mutually satisfying. Some couples find that the Creator of sexual union seems so near (as they enjoy one another with him) that they are able to pray together with their bodies still united after culminating their physical expression of love.

As God planned it, sexual intercourse was for marriage only. He knew all the potential harmful side-effects of the misuse of His gift outside marriage – which is the reason He forbade its use except within marriage.

Accepting, with gratitude, that God has given sex as something sure and pleasurable, we still have to answer the question, 'What *is* the purpose of sexual union?'

7. What is 'It' About?

To my surprise I could see my husband nodding with agreement and obvious pleasure at a tape of folk music I was playing.

'Funny!' I thought. 'He doesn't usually like folk.'

I drew nearer to find out the words of the song which was fascinating him. It was sung by Tom Paxton,

'When we were good she had her way with me.
She'd simply stay with me,
And make my whole day ring.
When we were good she'd make the nights go fast;
She'd put out the lights so fast,
She made my body sing.
Oh! She knew me inside out.
Oh! She made my senses shout. . . .'

The joy of sexual union was coming over through this, sung beautifully and reverently. Out of the different reasons why God gave sexual intercourse within marriage, perhaps the most obvious one is so that a couple could produce children, the fruit of their mutual love. While two bodies 'sing' in harmony (as in the song) a new life is being created out of their duet.

Yet, even something as seemingly simple as this may lead to unexpected problems, as Liz found,

'I thought that a wife should expect sex every night. When, after being married a few weeks, I was turned away from night after night with not even a kiss or cuddle, I felt I was not loved any more.

'If only I could have asked my husband – but any question was only briefly answered, so no more questions were asked.

'Much later I discovered the reason. I had always wanted children, and after a year of marriage we decided to stop contraception. I expected to become pregnant immediately, so when nothing happened I began to take my temperature in the mornings to discover when I ovulated.

Then, triumphantly, I would announce, 'This is the best night for it.'

'That would guarantee to turn my husband away, and I assumed this was deliberate.

'Finally, one night he quietly blurted out, "I can't just turn it on to order like that. . . ."'

'I had never understood his side of things before that.

'After that, in prayer, I just left this matter with God. *He* would know which ovum of mine he wanted to make into his child, and *he* could make my husband want me at just the right moment. I had immediate peace about this, and within three months conceived our first baby.'

The Old Testament writers often speak of the joy and privilege of having children, and of the tragedy of childlessness. God's command to Adam and Eve was, 'Be fruitful and multiply and subdue the earth.'

The Psalmist is enthusiastic about large families. In one psalm, the man who is truly happy is described as having so many children that they are like arrows *filling* his quiver. The next psalm in the Bible speaks of God's blessing upon the man who has a wife who is like a fruitful vine : their children are described as olive shoots around their table.

'Whatever is wrong with me?' I wonder, as I read these Bible passages.

The pictures conjured up in *my* mind are those from children's nursery rhyme books of the 'Old Woman who lived in a shoe, and who had so many children she didn't know what to do.'

The other haunting, unforgettable pictures are from the television and are of large families starving in refugee camps in Biafra, Bangladesh and Ethiopia. I cannot erase the memory of the mother of ten children piteously pleading for help for her dying baby cradled in her arms, and sucking feebly at her empty breasts. Help is being *refused* : she is being turned away : help is in such limited supply that only the babies with a good chance of survival can be cared for. The rest have to be left to die.

How does this fit in with the Psalmist's enthusiasm, and encouragement to a couple to produce as many children as they can? The cultural situation is very different today from that in Old Testament times. Then, a family's wealth lay in the potential of its children : now, an over-abundance of children, in a world of limited resources, may lead to a family's poverty.

It's easy to notice some of the Bible, and to ignore other parts. The command instructing Adam and Eve to produce children, also told them to be responsible people, 'Be fruitful and multiply, and fill the earth, *and subdue it. . . .*' Man was to learn to control the earth.

By the twentieth century, we can argue, 'Man has made a mess of this !'

He has misused many of the world's resources; selfishly depleted others; upset the balance of nature; and polluted the earth. One thing which he *can* do to try and minimize the ill-effects of his actions, is to control the tremendous world-wide population explosion, and prevent the chaos and unnecessary suffering that large families would bring to today's world. The Old Testament situation no longer applies today.

Each Christian married couple must thoughtfully and prayerfully seek God's guidance about the size of their family. The threats of world-wide over-population, and decreasing resources must be *seriously* considered. It must not be dismissed with a carefree, 'Tomorrow we'll see about it . . .', and meanwhile today another unplanned child is conceived; and eventually, out of laziness and failure to think, a whole unplanned tribe is brought into the world.

No Christian can judge another on this matter. God may guide one couple responsibly to produce eight children, and he may guide another to conceive none of their own but to adopt the unwanted children of others. In all matters of Christian conduct, God's will must receive priority. He does not guide everyone in a stereotyped manner.

Since a normal part of marriage is that children should be brought into the family, I disagree with those who say,

'We've tried for years to have a baby . . .' and when I ask, 'Have you been to the doctor?', reply

'No . . . it *must* be God's will for us to be childless.'

I believe that God has given knowledge and skills to doctors today so that couples who are childless find that medical aid can enable them to conceive a baby of their own. To me subfertility (or infertility) should receive medical treatment as much as a chronic cough. It is no more God's will for me to fail to seek treatment for infertility than it would be for tuberculosis.

I also believe that God has given modern medicine to enable couples to plan the size of their families, and to limit their children to the number which they feel God wants them to have. Here God often guides through prayerful commonsense. A couple may prayerfully consider, 'In the light of the world-wide situation, our financial position, our ability to cope with children, the size of our house – how many children should we have?'

God rarely guides as easily as the young mother who took Jesus' rebuke to the disciples, 'Let the children come . . . and do not stop them,' as his word to her to have another baby.

Each couple intending to limit the size of their family should talk frankly to a trained person about which method of family planning is right for them. The matter is controversial, even amongst Christian doctors, and so the layman cannot usually find a simple answer. He must, for himself, decide what is right.

God does not expect us to use available contraception because we are too lazy and too selfish to be bothered to rear any children. On the other hand, he may fail to give a couple children, or lead them to have no family, deliberately because he has some other purpose for their time and energies. He may equally lead them to foster or adopt children.

The whole matter is one in which a couple must stand before God, seeking His will and His glory. As I seek God's will for my life, so I must remember that I must on no account judge my brother if the Holy Spirit leads him in a different way. We are answerable to God. We have not

54

been appointed judges of our fellow-Christians in this matter.

The Christian may find himself seeking a balance between two extreme views, 'Sex in marriage should be practised *only* in order to conceive children! and 'Intercourse is natural and right for us . . . but *we never want* any children!'

Each of these extreme views has taken part of God's truth and used it in a way which distorts the Bible's teaching. While the Bible teaches that part of the meaning of sexual intercourse is that married couples should have children, it does not teach that this is the only purpose for which God gave sexual union within marriage.

In Genesis, and in Jesus' mention of a man and a woman becoming 'one flesh' in sexual intercourse, there is no mention of children. The Apostle Paul teaches very clearly, 'Because of the temptation to immorality, each man should have his own wife, and each woman her own husband . . .'

He also says, 'The husband should give to his wife her conjugal rights, and likewise the wife to her husband.'

This, and similar Bible teachings, make it clear that sexual intercourse was designed by God, not only to produce children but also to enable men and women to use their natural sexual desires in the right way. For this to be practical in experience, a married couple must find one another physically desirable. A 'sexual magnetism' should exist which attracts one to the other. If this element is lacking in marriage, then sexual union may be a cold, mechanical affair.

Some Christians run into trouble in this area. There is still a tendency for a Christian couple who are going out together to feel that the fact that they *are* going out, means that they must consider marriage.

Their non-Christian friends may adopt the attitude, 'I'll kiss her first, and ask her name afterwards.'

However, the Christian may take his boy-girl relationship intensely seriously; he may even feel that, having taken a girl out for some length of time, he is honour-bound to marry her. He may feel sure that, because they are both committed Christians, marriage is bound to be 'all right' for them. In such a relationship, the vital factor of sexual attraction may be missing. The couple may be tragically unaware of this fact, and even fail to realize that it may be very important to their future.

A 'friendship-marriage' may exist, in which sexual intercourse is not very important to either partner. The couple may be happy and find this is no problem. It may never be a problem to them. However, they may suddenly find they are catapulted into the nightmare of a marriage which is being shaken at its foundations and collapsing.

Paul writes that marriage was to be entered into 'because of the temptation to immorality'. If a couple marry, and do not find one another sexually attractive, then this clause is not fulfilled. If one of the partners meets someone else who is sexually very attractive, then the stability of a secure marriage is not there as the preventative that Paul recommended. One partner may be so thrown off-balance that he may be deafened to the voice of his conscience and may commit adultery. Even if events do not go as far as this, his eyes will have been opened to sexual attraction in another person, and he will realize the shattering truth, that he has married the wrong person – for very 'good reasons'. The tragedy of this situation, arising in the marriage between two Christians, can only be avoided, if as well as spiritual unity, the couple are sexually attracted to one another before they marry.

Jesus says that a man who 'looks after a woman to lust after her has sinned by committing adultery with her in his heart.' He does *not* say that sudden sexual desire is sin. He *does* say that allowing that desire to become a fantasy, and feeding it in one's thought-life, is sin.

The Apostle Paul speaks of marriage as desirable 'because of the temptation to immorality'. Were he to have lived in today's world of the exploitation of sex, he might have spoken even more forcefully. His words ring very true to those who find they are tempted sexually daily, and discover in their love for their marriage partner the preventative against sin which they need. The man who finds his wife sexually satisfying has no need for a fantasy sexual life, nor acts of immorality. The man who is in love with his wife sees *her* as he travels up the London Underground escalators past the advertisements of long, bare legs, bras, and trousers focusing on the crutch. He sees her in the sexually stimulating television advertisements. She is proving to be the preventative about which the Apostle Paul wrote.

A wife may fail her husband in this respect. She may be worn-out with caring for small children, and be so preoccupied with the family that she has forgotten her role as a sexual partner for her husband. She may not *deny* him : but she may fail to make herself attractive. When he is sexually stimulated by the world in which he lives, his mental picture of his drab wife, lifeless and uninteresting, may then be *no* preventative for him. Temptation to wander in a sexual fantasy world may become very hard for him to resist.

If he falls, and sins, his wife must in some measure share the responsibility for this. In a world of inflation, a woman may find it hard to feed and clothe the family. She might argue that she has insufficient money to make herself attractive to her husband. If money is short, then she *must* find other means of achieving the same end – surely no woman can fail to find some way of remaining attractive to the man she loves?

To write of a wife's role in such terms would have seemed almost immodest, or indecent, fifty years ago. Yet, with modern advertising techniques it may be more important to the maintenance of the marriages of Christians in the Western world, than some of us realize. A man and his wife need to stand together to cope with the psychological assaults of today's barrage of sexually stimulating material presented by the mass media.

Not only did God give man sexual intercourse as a means of procreation, and as a preventative, but also for pleasure.

In his goodness God has given mankind sexual fulfilment for the sheer joy it imparts. It expresses the committed completeness of the married couple, and their desire to give themselves wholly to one another, with no strings attached. Delight in sex was not invented in the twentieth century.

In the Old Testament, Abraham's wife, Sarah, knew that intercourse was to be enjoyed and not to be endured.

When she was told that in her old age she would become pregnant, her response was, 'After I have grown old, and my husband has grown old, shall I have *pleasure*?'

In other places in the Old Testament the word, which is here translated as 'pleasure', refers to the gratification of sexual desires. I presume from this that Sarah had known the delight of sexual intercourse.

The Old Testament comments on sexual pleasure in marriage as a normal occurrence. Abimilech was quick to spot that the way Isaac was fondling Rebekah was the way lovers behave, these were not the actions of a brother and sister, as he had been deceived into thinking.

A young married man was expected to bring sexual satisfaction to his wife. He was not called-up into the army for a year after he had married. Why? The reason given is so that he could 'cheer', or 'pleasure', or build a satisfying relationship with his wife.

I find the Old Testament down-to-earth and realistic. This young married couple were not expected to develop a mature relationship overnight. It was recognized that they would need *time* to cultivate, and work at building, a relationship that would last. It was implied that since marriage is the most important of human relationships, it was worth freeing the bridegroom from army service for a year, so that he could establish a solid foundation for his marriage.

It was realistically accepted that it is difficult for most people to adjust to two new relationships at the same time; therefore the bridegroom was set free to learn the role of husband before he adjusted to the role of soldier.

The attitude of 'waltz down the aisle in white and live happily ever after' does not fit into this realistic picture of having to work to *build* a marriage relationship.

Reading the Song of Solomon in the Old Testament, I see both sexual desire and fulfilment, presented without perversion or misuse. It shines as a unique and precious gift which God has given to mankind.

Within marriage it has been given for procreation, prevention, and pleasure. It forms a vital part of a developing marriage relationship.

If a marriage is not to become stagnant, how may it grow and mature?

8. A Growing Relationship

I was intrigued to meet her, efficient and attractively dressed, at her office at work. She was much more what I pictured a successful single business woman to be, than a wife.

'What has her husband done?' I was forced to ask myself.

There was obviously an ingredient in her marriage which was absent in the marriages of many Christian couples I knew.

She gave me a clue herself, as we chatted over a cup of coffee, 'Why don't you read *The Integrity of the Personality* by Anthony Storr?' she suggested. At the time I did not realize the insight into her own relationship that this book would give me.

I duly obtained, and read it, beginning to gain insight into the precious present that her husband had given her, a gift that few husbands would have thought of giving: one of more value than a diamond and ruby tiara.

Anthony Storr writes, 'I propose to call this final achievement "self-realization", by which I mean the fullest possible expression in life of the innate potentialities of the individual, the realization of his own uniqueness as a personality: and I also put forward the hypothesis that, consciously or unconsciously, every man is seeking this goal.'

He continues further on, 'I believe that the development of the individual and the maturity of his personal relationships proceed hand-in-hand, and that one cannot take place without the other. Self-realization is not an anti-social principle; it is firmly based on the fact that men need each other in order to be themselves, and that those people who succeed in achieving the greatest degree of independence and maturity are also those who have the most satisfactory relationships with others.'

He later says, 'Self-realization, so far as anyone ever achieves it, is manifested by the widest exercise of the individual's potentialities combined with the attainment of a mature relationship with others.'

Finally, 'if we are sufficiently fortunate in our partner, and if our relationship is a progressive thing, not merely a static achievement, we may approximate to a stage in which, because each fulfils the other's needs, each is also treated as a whole person by the other. Whereas formerly two people in love served only to complete what each felt to be lacking – now two whole people confront each other as individuals. The attainment of this stage of development is marked also by a diminution of the competitive striving so characteristic of young people who are not yet certain of themselves as men or women. . . . A happy marriage perhaps represents the ideal of human relationship – a setting in which each partner, while acknowledging the need of the other, feels free to be what he or she by nature is : a relationship in which instinct as well as intellect can find expression : in which giving and taking are equal : in which each accepts the other. . . .'

I was confronted by a Christian wife whose husband had given her the valuable gift of allowing her to 'realize' herself, and to exercise her potential to the full. Unlike some wives, she was not expected to be a kind of extension of her husband's personality (like the tail of a dog); she was encouraged to be a person in her own right. Her husband had not 'cocooned' her from the world in a nice little nest of a home away from life's realities. He had allowed her out of her home, to make an independent place for herself in the world. He had the insight to realize that this was vital for the woman he had married if she was to mature fully. He would be the first to admit that this would not apply to *every* wife, but it was important to his wife. I felt I was seeing a Christian marriage which was creative, and growing as God intended. Permanent domesticity would have crushed and stunted this woman, and repercussed negatively in her marriage. Her children received all the love and attention which they needed, and have not missed out.

There were many things I wanted to know about this particular marriage.

'What do you make of the clear teaching in the Bible,' I asked, 'where we are told, "Wives, be subject to your husbands, as to the Lord. For the husband is the head of the wife as Christ is the head of the Church"?'

Listening to her reply, I found our thoughts ran parallel. Neither of us interpreted this Bible teaching as meaning that the man who is going to fulfil his God-given role of being the 'head' of his wife, should be a husband who is stern and legalistic, of necessity suppressing his wife's personality. The Bible's picture of 'headship' does not, to either of us, depict dictatorship.

Christian husbands are told to love their wives as Christ loved the Church. The head of the Church, the Lord Jesus, draws and leads by love. His is the example Christian husbands are told to copy.

'If you agree that your husband is your "head", does that make you inferior?' I next wanted to know.

As I had expected, the attractive, fulfilled woman in front of me shook her head. I had rightly anticipated her reply, 'Why should that be so? The New Testament tells us that "in Christ there is neither male nor female" . . .'

Like her, I cannot convince myself that the Bible teaches that to be male is to be spiritually superior to one who is female. It was the female, Eve, who suggested that Adam should disobey God and taste the forbidden fruit in the Garden of Eden. However, she did not tie him up, and *force* the fruit into his mouth: he ate *willingly*, knowing he was doing wrong. The fact that he followed his wife's bad advice does not (to me) make him spiritually superior to her.

I believe that the Bible teaches that in the New Testament era in God's eyes both sexes are spiritually equal, and that each individual, regardless of sex, is of infinite value. With the coming of Christ, the Jewish concepts about woman's inferiority have been superseded.

While I believe that male and female are equal as

persons, yet when they become *partners* in a marriage, then they have different roles to fulfil. In most social institutions, someone usually has to have the final authority, even if it is rarely used. 'The buck stops here!' applies as much to marriage as to other areas of life. The Apostle Paul writes about this : 'I want you to understand that the head of every man is Christ, the head of a woman is her husband, and the head of Christ is God.'

This seems to teach that God has instituted a chain of authority. We know from other parts of the Bible that Christ *willingly* submitted to God's authority; so the husband submits to Christ; the wife to the husband; and children to their parents.

A son is not made inferior to his father because he submits to his authority. Why then should some deduce that a wife is inferior to her husband if she gives him the final authority in their marriage relationship?

To many of us, the one who carries any 'authority' is assumed to be 'superior' to others not carrying such authority. Perhaps we need to re-examine our reasoning. Why should we assume that a wife is made of 'less value' when she submits to her husband's authority? Jesus *knew* He was not inferior to his Father; he said, 'I and my Father are one . . .'

However, as a Son, working in partnership, and in this role, in submission to his Father, he said in Gethsemane, 'Nevertheless . . . your will done.'

Submission to his Father did not decrease Jesus' value. He was not made inferior when He submitted to his Father's authority.

In God's plan for his chain of authority, it is essential for there to be willingness on the part of those taking part, in carrying out his pattern. God, the Father, did not force his Son to submit to his authority. Jesus submitted willingly, even though it was tremendously costly at times. God never over-rides man's free will, forcing him into rebellious submission. In the same way no Christian husband should *force* his wife to submit to his wishes. He must lead in love, treating his wife as a partner who is as intelligent as he is.

This is not easy for everyone to accept. Some would question, 'What happens if by nature a man is the recessive partner, and the wife dominant? Surely such a wife should take the lead? Isn't this the reason her husband chose her to be his partner in the first place? He wanted someone who'd shoulder the responsibility with which he felt he could not cope.'

Such a situation is one which the couple concerned must prayerfully face up to and frankly discuss. As Christians in this, as in all matters of life, their final authority must be God's teaching. Whether they like it or not, the Bible clearly states that the husband is the 'head' of the wife. Neither the Church, nor the Victorians, nor male chauvinists invented this teaching! If we accept the Bible as authoritative, we have to accept this teaching.

We tend to misconstrue and misinterpret to suit our own ideas. The Bible does *not* say that the man who is 'head' of his wife makes all decisions himself; never delegates any responsibility; and never discusses matters with his wife, treating her as a rational being. The husband is ultimately responsible for decisions – but this is no reason for him failing to give this responsibility to his wife where appropriate. She then acts on his behalf.

The extent of delegation of responsibility must vary from couple to couple. At one extreme is the wife who is incapable of deciding more than domestic details. She is only too thankful for her husband to decide everything. At the other extreme I remember a highly competent wife of a man in the armed services, who burst out at me, 'How *can* he decide when he's away abroad at his work most of the time? He's never there when most decisions have to be taken. He trusts me to decide in his absence, and always backs me up in what I felt should be done!' She carried a slight resentment against the Christian community in which she lived, since she felt they condemned her for 'wearing the trousers' in her marriage.

The recurring problem unmarried people seem to ask about marriage is, 'Suppose the couple discuss something . . . and disagree . . . what then?' However, in chatting to married Christian couples, it becomes obvious that this

64

is rarely a *practical* problem. In the final analysis, the answer is that the husband has the last word, and his decision is followed if the couple cannot agree. This may be difficult for some wives to accept, if they are used to making decisions involving other people's lives in their professional work. If such a wife interprets the Bible as I do, then she will have mentally to agree to disagree with her husband at times, and graciously to do as he wants. If his plan fails, she must refrain from a critical or tactless, 'I told you so . . . you should have listened. . . .'

The alternative is for her to ignore those Bible teachings which she does not particularly like – but dare she *start* doing this? Once she starts picking and choosing which parts of the Bible she will accept, and which reject, where does she stop?

At one extreme may be a couple in which the husband leaves his wife to organize practically everything. He is caricatured by the words, 'My wife makes all the small decisions about moving house and the children's education; while I make the big decision like which party we will vote for. . . .'

There may be many variations in the practical outworking of a relationship in which the husband is not by nature a planner, or able to foresee the repercussions of any course of action. For in this partnership, at rockbottom, the husband is still responsible to God for the decisions his wife makes with the authority he has delegated to her.

Unfortunately the fact that the husband is the 'head' of the wife, does not confer on him immunity from making mistakes! He is as much in need of the guidance of the Holy Spirit in the home as when preaching in church.

Perhaps he is more in need of the power and infilling of the Holy Spirit when his wife is out shopping; he may be at the end of his tether with baby screaming, telephone ringing, and food burning. He may need the Holy Spirit's help more in this situation than when he is in the pulpit.

What happens when a husband makes the wrong decision? He may long for the loving acceptance and forgiveness by his wife similar to that which he receives from God. Instead he may receive only silent implied criticism, or the muttered resentful, 'I could have told you so. . . .'

The wife who explodes in such a situation, causing a row, may not always have done the wrong thing. The Bible does not teach that anger is always wrong. 'Be angry and sin not' implies that there can be a right use of anger. Anger may be used creatively in a marriage to enable partners to understand one another's deepest feelings, thoughts, and resentments. Their expression, instead of repression, can open a door to deeper understanding and communication.

The Bible has some very difficult things to teach about the way in which God wants a husband to treat his wife, teachings which may seem impossibly idealistic to the average, realistic man.

'Husbands, love your wives, as Christ loved the Church and gave himself up for her. . . .'

'Husbands should love their wives as their own bodies. He who loves his wife loves himself. For no man ever hates his own flesh, but nourishes and cherishes it, as Christ does the Church.' And 'Let each one of you love his wife as himself.'

While the mass media sometimes equate male love with weakness, the Bible depicts real love as something masculine, strong and powerful. It is masculine for a man to show tenderness and deep affection for his wife; this is not effeminate behaviour. It may be costly for a husband to free his wife, so that she can develop and mature fully in her own right. To do so, he needs to 'love his wife as himself' in reality.

Jesus loved the Church despite her faults and failings; like Him a Christian husband is to go on loving his wife even when she is most unlovable and has let him down badly and perhaps repeatedly. This requires an unconditional, God-given love, which springs from an effort of the will.

We may be daunted by the roles the Bible teaches us we are to play in our marriages. It may seem far above us, and beyond our reach. We are all normal, weak human beings. Yet God wants us to attain the highest possible for us.

A mature marriage relationship does not suddenly blossom into flowers with the exchange of wedding rings and vows. It is something into which we grow.

As we allow the Holy Spirit to fill and control our married lives, he will gradually change us, with all our imperfections, and transform us into the people he wants us to be.

One of the greatest gifts and the deepest expressions of love a husband can give to his wife, is to allow her to develop fully as a person in her own right. It will be costly. Not every husband is prepared to love his wife enough to allow this to happen. Dare it be said that he is then *disobeying* his Master's command, 'Love your wives, as Christ loved the Church, and gave himself up for her....'?

9. The 'Submissive' Wife

'Things ain't wot they used to be!' cheerfully sings one twentieth century wife, grateful for so many changes, and her world of mass communications and instant everything. She would not have liked the kind of life her grandmothers led.

Yet, the fact that things are changing means that many wives are having to redefine their roles in marriage and in society. The Christian wife is not isolated and living in a community exempt from these changes. She is having to sort out how these changes in society affect her both as a Christian and as a wife. She finds this difficult.

Granny's generation of wives were legally secure. Things have changed. Since the Divorce Reform Act of 1969, a modern wife can be divorced without consent. She may feel insecure, if her marriage relationship is unstable.

When Granny was young, she did not think it unusual for a wife to face extreme anxiety and even severe poverty if the family ran into trouble. The modern wife, however, *expects* the welfare state to look after her, and her family, when things go wrong. She tends to grumble that enough is not done for her when she needs help from the State.

She does not expect a drop in her standard of living, but rather that it should rise, regardless of the effort she and her husband make. She would like her husband to do less work for more pay.

A continuous, remorseless rise in the cost of living, coupled with a desire to maintain a certain standard of living has forced many wives to go out to work. They may, by working, be able to prevent a fall in their standard. Frustratingly, despite hard work, and due to inflation they are unable to rise any higher. They are working hard only to maintain the *status quo*.

Granny, who chatted regularly to her neighbours, would be horrified at the plight of some of her granddaughters. She would never have envisaged a wife who was so lonely and bored in an industrial suburb, a modern housing estate, or a high-rise flat, that she felt she had to flee from home to find company and friends by going out to work.

Granny would never have imagined that her great-great-grandchildren might be cared for day by day, by a nursery, or a child-minder, so that mother could work from choice and not always from necessity. Nor could she have imagined that this could have led to a state of affairs where a wife spent minimal time in the kitchen : modern labour-saving devices, and instant foods reducing the amount of time needed for domestic chores.

Her granddaughters marry younger than she would have. Therefore, they tend to wait for a few years before having their first baby. A couple who are deeply in love tend to be encouraged to marry. Granny would have saved for her home, and waited a few years. Her grand-children argue that even if they wait, and save, their savings will depreciate so rapidly that the wait will not have been worthwhile. They are probably right. On marriage Granny expected to stop work, to be a full-time housewife. Her granddaughters often expect to continue working at least until the first child is born. They then face the difficult problem of budgeting on one person's earnings, instead of two, at a time when the additional third mouth to feed means they need more and not less money. Such a wife has to be careful not to live beyond her income. She may have to lower her standard of living or may get caught up with buying on the 'never-never' system. She may enter marriage unprepared for the problems which will loom up menacingly to confront her. She may have been prepared for married life as Granny knew it, and suddenly find herself precipitated into an unexpected, lonely new world in a materialistic society.

A Christian bride, like others, may enter marriage in a happy daze, totally unaware and unprepared for the realities of twentieth century life which lie ahead.

The attitude, 'We are both Christians; therefore everything will automatically be all right,' does not prepare a couple for the fact that a successful marriage is one which has been worked hard on. God *does* wonderfully help a couple who ask for His help : but He expects them to try their human best.

The Christian wife, who intends to 'cleave to' her husband, may still, because she is a normal human being, find it hard to separate herself from parents and her family. Like other wives she faces the temptation to 'run home to mum' when things start to go wrong. Similarly, her husband may face difficulty in finding in his wife all that he used to obtain from his mother. His wife has to learn to be to him wife, mother, lover, and friend. This may be difficult for both.

Christians are not immune to the changed role wives play in society today, nor to the changes in role that marriage brings to a woman. They cannot live in a Christian ghetto, as if it were still the nineteenth century. Today's Christians must be people of today – who have found the Bible's relevance for today.

Christians, like other wives, can feel that their self-identity has never been established. They, like some wives, may also feel that their 'real self' has been submerged under a sea of housework, and the endless work involved in bringing up children. 'Home' may have become a prison from which they feel there is no hope of escape, except for brief visits to church or relatives. Professional training and intellectual potential may appear wasted to them as they mechanically hang out endless lines of wet clothes to dry, feeling their brains are going down the drain with the washing-up water.

Loneliness in talking to no one but pre-school children from dawn to dusk may be accentuated by having only the unreal world of the television and radio as 'adult company' by day. Of course, prayer and the 'practice of the presence of God' help a Christian – but she is still humanly lonely. If husbands then spend evenings in church activities, some of these Christian wives may feel desolate. They may sink into a kind of apathy, in which they lose their sense of identity as real people, who matter. Even the theoretical knowledge that God knows and loves them loses meaning, since they are unrecognized as humans by fellow-humans.

If such a wife is hit with the shock of sudden 'self-realization', she may find she is rebelling against accepted marriage roles. She may feel these have dictated that the wife should be 'nothing', while the husband is 'fulfilled' and has 'everything'. She may rebel vigorously and violently.

Of course, many wives are unperturbed by all these factors. They find the rebels impossible to understand. They are blessed to be happy and content in running a home and bringing up children. They find identity and self-realization in being wives and mothers. For them, domesticity is completely fulfilling.

Some other wives feel that their sole hope for survival as persons is to spend at least part of the day away from home. This is the only way in which they can preserve the self-identity vital to their existence, and the full Christian life they feel God intended them to have. They cannot experience the 'abundant life' which Jesus offers them, in a confined, solitary high-rise flat with labour-saving devices which enable housework to be finished in a few hours. Some are able to combine housework with an outside job, and find no apparent ill-effects in their family : on the contrary, because the quality of their own lives is enhanced, this in turn enriches their marriage and family life. The family benefits from a fulfilled, instead of a frustrated, mother.

Because today's women are facing problems in sorting out their roles and identity in marriage in a changing society, today's husbands need special wisdom from God, to understand the needs of the individual woman they have married. No two women are alike. No two women have similar needs or problems.

The woman who cries in desperation, 'I'm *me*. . . . I'm not an extension of *you*. . . . Please help me to find and to be true to myself!', is not helped by a shrugged reply, 'Why can't you be happy to run your house as my Mum did. . . . What ever are you going on and on about this for. . . .'

71

Where necessary, an understanding husband may not only free his wife from full-time domesticity to serve the community, and retain her self-identity and self-respect. He may go even further by saying, 'If *she's* sharing the breadwinning, then there's no real reason why I shouldn't share the housework,' as he rolls up his sleeves to take on some of the heavier chores.

The Christian wife who feels that her husband treats her as a *person* (and not a thing) will not find New Testament teachings hard to follow. She will willingly accept such a husband as her 'head'. She will not resent Bible teaching like 'Wives, be submissive to your husbands,' and 'Wives, be subject to your husbands, as is fitting in the Lord.'

She will not find it hard to 'submit' to such a husband. These words will *not* be a bitter pill, the swallowing of which is to be avoided if at all possible. She will be willing for what seems humanly impossible.

If a Christian wife finds that she is unwilling to 'submit' to her husband, then what can she do? The Bible gives her no choice! She is given a command to obey.

Her cry may have to be very elementary, 'God, make me willing to be made willing to submit to him . . . whatever "submission" really means.'

As the Holy Spirit changes many aspects of our lives, He is able to change the attitude of the wife, who honestly desires to follow God's command, but cannot in her own strength.

Submission led Jesus to the Cross. For some Christian wives, 'submission' to their husbands may be costly; but in God's hands it may both be possible and be fruitful in their lives.

Since 'submission' is an attitude of mind and will, it neither means that a woman is used freely as a sexual object; nor that she is the slave of her husband; nor that she loses her identity. Where she truly loves her husband, 'submission' becomes part of a total caring, developing relationship, of interdependence.

10. Now We are Three Plus

'Who ever wrote that daft song?' my husband asked.

I was paying little attention to his words, my ears intent on catching yet another wail from the baby upstairs.

'Which one, darling?' I vaguely replied.

'You know, that one which was your favourite when we were still engaged. . . .'

'Oh! That one that goes "When the children are asleep, we'll sit and dream. . . ."?' As an engaged couple, that song had captivated us when we used to cuddle by the fire, picturing the cosy bliss conjured up by such words and music.

He nodded pensively, 'I bet it was composed by a bachelor, who had never had any children of his own!'

He eyed the clock, its hands indicating it was time *we* went to sleep.

'The trouble is, since the babies arrived, there hasn't been any time even to sit : let alone time to dream. . . .'

I knew he was objectively stating a fact. He had wanted and loved our children as much as I did. He did not resent the time they consumed. The trouble was that they needed so much *time*, that there was little left for one another. Even if we found a free hour to be together, we tended to be so tired we wanted to collapse in an armchair to recuperate.

Our problem was a common one. When Pam married, she found she was torn in two between her husband and the baby, who was born a year after marriage. Mike expected her, as the 'ideal wife', to sit and have her evening meal with *him* at 6.00 p.m. on the dot. This was the time the baby could be guaranteed to be crying to be fed. Pam had not adapted her baby's feeding routine to fit in with her husband's desire for her presence at the evening meal, and so she found this meal almost impossible to

73

tolerate. Who came first: her husband or her wailing infant?

Liz too found problems in sharing herself between her husband and children.

'For years, prior to my marriage I had been advising mothers (in my capacity as a Health Visitor) to be careful to give their husbands their rightful place and not to ignore them once children arrived. I thought I was being careful to observe this myself.

'One day, when the children were about two and four years old, my mother-in-law came to stay. I went upstairs to put the children to bed.

'My husband called up after me, "That programme which you wanted to see is on at 7 o'clock."

'OK love!' I shouted back.

'Due to delays with the children, I didn't re-appear until about 7.15 p.m. My husband was furious with me.

'I justified my position, "But I had so many things to do for the children. I couldn't get down sooner. *Anyway*, it's *me* who wanted to see that programme, so I'm only denying myself!"

'Deep silent gloom settled over my husband. Later on, in the kitchen, I asked my mother-in-law for advice, "What did you make of all that, mother? Was I wrong?"

'Back came the surprising, unexpected reply, "I think you were! You always put the children first, don't you? Your husband was wanting to please you, and you didn't even give him the chance to do so, did you?"

'Having got over the shock of her reply, I began to examine my behaviour more carefully. I reluctantly realized that she had spoken the truth.'

Early marriage is usually a time of deep satisfaction to a couple. They rejoice in having discovered one another; as they interact they feel that each is complementing the deficiencies of the other. They bask in a rosy glow of mutual appreciation.

The later shocks of reality may lead to disenchantment. Reality is forced on a couple by the arrival of the first baby. The wife is no longer free and available whenever her husband wants her. She is tied to the baby, and no longer able to go out with him at any time, sharing the activities they had previously enjoyed together.

Lack of availability and freedom may be coupled with exhaustion. She may be too tired, from endless broken nights, and demoralizing days, to manage to raise more than a faint flicker of interest in her husband's activities. If he feels that babies are exclusively objects for women to take care of, then she may become progressively tired due to no relief from 'baby-duty'. The husband who gives his wife a 'day off from nappy changing' on Sunday, may be helping his wife in more ways than he realizes.

Meg and Don (a theoretical couple and the only "theoretical couple" in this book) were blissfully happy in their marriage. Both were delighted when Meg announced her first pregnancy, but were totally unprepared for the disruption that an eight-pound lovable bundle of a baby could make to their well-planned daily routine.

Meg stopped work to have and look after the baby and their income dropped. She had to live at a lower standard than the television implied she should, and learnt to go without small luxuries she had previously enjoyed. She did not mind, because she loved her baby and wanted to do all that she thought a mother should for her children. She felt they were a precious gift and trust given by God. When the novelty of being at home all day had worn off, she found she was lonely and bored. Her baby slept nearly all day, and required minimal attention when he was tiny.

For some reason, however hard Meg tried to prevent it, the baby always seemed to be in the middle of his evening feed, when Don arrived home in the evening. The adults' meal had to be delayed. The cosy twosome, previously enjoyed, was now broken.

They both dearly loved their baby . . . but they wished he wouldn't decide to cry at night, just at the moment when they were beginning to enjoy one another sexually. By the time Meg had settled the baby, Don was fast asleep. Broken nights were beginning to make the couple irritable. Unconsciously, Don found he was beginning to slightly resent the large share of Meg that the baby had taken away from him.

At this stage, it may be helpful for a couple to look at their marriage through fresh eyes : to reassess the situation : to try and work out how they should react and cope with the new pressures of having a third member introduced into their family.

A tiny seed of separation may have unknowingly been sown by the arrival of their baby.

Unless the growth of this seed is checked quickly, roots may begin to sprout, grow, become established, finally flourishing in the case of a couple whose children have been allowed to push them apart.

The tiny seed of resentment in Don's heart may flourish, so that he begins to feel that his wife is too busy to give him any time. He may gradually feel unwanted (except as the odd job man around the house), and even that his wife no longer loves him as she used to. If pushed to an extreme, he may seek fulfilment in ceaseless activity, or reassurance through relationships which take him away from his wife.

The wife may feel that she is no longer of interest as a person to her husband (and she may have allowed herself to become so unattractive by neglect that he finds it hard to be interested in her !). She may be conscious that she is very tired, and looks a mess, and that life tends to have swamped her. She has no physical, mental or emotional energy for her husband. A tiny seed may have been sown, making her feel that she is no longer wanted by her husband as she once was : that domesticity and babies are all that her life can now be expected to contain.

Radical stocktaking of a marriage can transform such a potentially dangerous situation. If a couple can face up to what *has* happened, or what *might* happen, they can then together determine to work to prevent the seed of trouble from developing into a destructive plant.

On a practical level, relatives, baby-sitters and friends can often transform this situation. If a couple can recognize their need to maintain their closeness to one another, and to preserve their unique relationship, they may be able to find someone who will occasionally look after their children, so that they can be alone together as 'Don and Meg . . . Mr. and Mrs.' instead of always being 'Mum and Dad . . . child-rearers.'

If it is impossible for them to get away alone together, then they must cherish the joy of togetherness in the middle of the family. Small gestures and looks come to count in such situations. Little acts of caring, showing that each partner has noticed and appreciates the other, become very precious. The wife who bothers to change and dress attractively for her husband's homecoming on an ordinary evening; the husband who brings home even a single flower to his wife; these actions express more eloquently than words that, 'Even though there's no time to spend alone telling you this, I want you to know that I feel just the same about you as I always have. . . .' Continued expressed or indicated love and mutual caring should prevent the arrival of a baby into the family from threatening the security of either of the partners.

The advent of a baby brings other problems which may begin to drive a wedge between previously happy partners. They may not have the same ideas about how children should be brought up. The couple who 'fall in love' rarely sit in the sunset, in a dream world, discussing the *discipline* of the children they long one day to produce. Couples coming from differing backgrounds will have widely differing ideas, and may not realize this until the first problem with the first baby arises. Don and Meg were no exception.

As the baby became a toddler the couple found they disagreed on discipline. Because Meg was home all day she tended to be stricter than Don. He wanted his children to have greater freedom of expression. They had to compromise, and learn not to disagree in front of the child. They discovered that if they were not careful, he would play one of them off against the other. It would have been easy for them to allow their disagreement to separate them and spoil their love for each other.

Such disagreement needs to be faced openly, and sorted

out between the couple. As Christian parents, we must determine just *how* God intends us to bring up our children. Unless we form a united front, this difference of opinion can form a nagging root of disagreement which will continually crop up. Such a basic disagreement will become worse (not better) as our children reach adolescence, so we must face it earlier rather than later in our marriage relationship.

The advent of a baby may tend not only to separate some couples (although others will find themselves more closely united) but it may also cause havoc with the patterns of life of some Christians. Those who have tended to mould their lives and practices on the way that other Christians live, may find that they are now at a loss, because they can no longer live as they used to.

Meg soon realized that, as a Christian, her 'spiritual life' had also been totally disrupted. She had always felt it was vital for her to get up early to read her Bible and pray before breakfast. She had assumed that this was essential if she was going to continue to be a Christian. The arrival of the baby, with consequent broken nights, meant that often she overslept, and missed her morning time of communion with God. She began to feel very guilty over this. If she sat down, later on in the day, to try and read her Bible, she found it difficult to concentrate. If she was very tired, she tended to fall asleep, Bible on her knee.

This total disruption of her neatly-organized 'spiritual life' forced her to take stock of the situation. She realized that she had perhaps been *too* organized before. Regular Bible reading programmes, and rigid daily prayer lists no longer fitted into her irregular programme of motherhood. She found a startling and precious discovery as she was forced by circumstances to develop a totally new approach to maintaining her relationship with God.

Instead of setting aside a fixed time of day to be 'God's time', she learnt to snatch any odd quiet minutes to focus her attention upon God. She learnt how to be with God at any time and in any place. She realized that the *quality* of such times was of more value than *quantity*.

Five minutes of deep communion with God was more precious to her now then her former twenty minutes, which she had because of her up-bringing felt 'ought to be spent in prayer'. She had been conditioned to believe that unless she spent time with God in the morning, then the day was bound to be a disaster : 'full of sin and failure'. Experience was proving the fallacy of such conditioning.

She learnt to snatch any odd minutes and quickly read a few verses of the Bible; then she would think, and re-think about those Bible verses, as she never had before, while she washed the dishes, and cleaned the windows. She found that in practice she was actually spending *more* time thinking about the Bible, its teaching and implications in her life, than she had ever before.

All this did not happen out of the blue. It was the result of a determined effort of her will. She made an effort to switch her thoughts on to God and to learn to relate to Him throughout the day. However, this effort was infinitely worth while, as she experienced a deepening awareness of God's reality in many aspects of life instead of only in the time she previously had set aside for Him before breakfast. Perhaps before she had, without realizing it, finished her prayer-time by unconsciously saying, 'Goodbye God ! See you again tomorrow morning !'

Don found it easier to maintain his previous habits of prayer and Bible reading. However, he discovered that one of his children woke early, and had a habit of seeking his praying father for a private early morning cuddle.

He could have approached this one of two ways. Either he could have gently and lovingly said, 'Right now, Jim, I'm spending some time with God . . . I'll be with you in half an hour . . .' This would have been realistic only if Jim did not have to get to school and his father had no pressure to be at work on time.

Alternatively he could have thought, 'I love you, Jimmy . . . to receive a child is in some ways to receive Christ himself. Come on into my arms . . .' However, having done this, he would not have resolved his practical problem of *when* in a busy day he will find time to be alone with God.

Perhaps no father ever resolves this problem completely. I have happy memories of two fathers who crashed head-on in a holiday centre as they *crawled* past their children's rooms, so as not to be spotted from the windows as they went to seek time alone with God. They were so busy avoiding detection from the windows that neither noticed the other heading his way.

Don and Meg also found that it was very hard to find time to pray together. They could never *find* time, they had to *make* it. They knew in their heart of hearts that they should try and pray as a couple to their heavenly Father. Lack of time, and the constant demands of their toddlers made it easy in practice for weeks to go past during which they had not prayed together, other than a sort of 'God bless . . .' routine in bed at night as they fell asleep.

The sole solution to this, they found, was to snatch any odd quiet unplanned moments that unexpectedly arose . . . the children suddenly might be engrossed in a harmless project and there were the precious minutes they needed. They also learnt how to pray together in the middle of family chaos. As long as the children were happy, and safe, they learnt to pray together in the middle of the kitchen, realizing that the calm of a cathedral with its sense of God's majesty was not to be theirs for a few years! They were sure that Jesus, whose home had been incredibly cramped, would understand if they seemed to be praying in the 'wrong place' : and had not the Bible told them to 'pray at all times'?

As their family increased to three children, Meg and Don longed that their children should grow up to know God for themselves. They both tried to bring God into everyday life, and to talk about Him naturally to the children as relevant situations arose. They longed that the quality of their lives would be such that their children should 'catch', or 'be infected' by, Christianity from their parents, rather than feel indoctrinated by them. They did not want their children to feel that religion had been rammed down their throats, along with vitamins and iron. They wanted Christianity to be to their children a relationship with God rather than a religious system.

Because other Christian families practised what was referred to as 'Family Prayers', Don and Meg struggled to bring this alive in their home. They found it a tremendous problem! It seemed every effort of theirs was doomed to dismal failure. By the time the youngest child could understand anything, the eldest was heard to murmur that he was 'bored by all that baby stuff'. Any effort to raise the intellectual level meant the youngest child was not listening. They could have *forced* their children to sit and listen to anything Don wanted to teach, but were frightened their children might learn a boring system of beliefs, and never meet the Person who alone makes Christianity relevant.

To find a time when the family was together was a very practical problem. Don left early for work, and their oldest child was often out in the evenings. They finally abandoned efforts to conduct united, daily 'family prayers'. Instead, they read the Bible and prayed with each child individually at night. They felt slightly guilty, and that they were failing the slogan, 'The family that prays together stays together.' They prayed – but not 'together'. After a few years like this, their children began to pray and read their Bibles for themselves, and to turn to God in daily needs and problem situations.

Other families might have said that Don and Meg had been wrong. They would have emphasized that every Christian family must learn to worship together as a family. They would have stressed the need to *fight* hard to overcome all obstacles, so that it was possible for the family to worship together at home, even if only for a few minutes. Some other families would have not allowed themselves to be defeated by these problems. Some have battled through and found their own solutions – individual solutions, geared to the individual family unit. They reckon the fight to have been infinitely worth while.

Church life posed an even greater problem. It seemed

to Don and Meg to separate rather than unite the family. It did not lead them as a family unit to experience and worship God together but seemed rather to encourage isolation and individuality. William Barclay's definition of worship was not made possible for them in church; worship, he says, is 'to confess and to experience the supreme worth of God. It is through some means or other to find the presence of God, and through that discovery to find inspiration and the strength to live a life which is fit for the presence of God'.

The children were quick to notice that this institution, 'The church', made Dad or Mum be absent from the family circle some evenings every week : often when Dad was needed to help with maths homework ! The eldest child was separated even more from the family when he joined the church youth group. Don and Meg were glad that their children were learning independence – but deep down they longed for a church which would stabilize and deepen their family unit.

Sunday morning services rarely satisfied the whole family. The children enjoyed 'family services' but the parents were left feeling spiritually hungry. They had gone longing to meet God : but all too often met only fellow Christians. Normal services bored the children, and the parents were so busy keeping them quiet that they themselves could neither worship nor listen properly to the sermon. They felt that others in the church disapproved of the children's presence, because their fidgeting, dropping their collection, and playing with books, distracted from worship, and from the preacher during the sermon.

Don and Meg began to attend church less and less because they felt unwelcome with their children. Not only this, but they were concerned lest boredom with 'church' would turn their children away from *God*. They wanted their children to learn Christianity, not 'churchianity'.

Other Christian families would have reacted quite differently. Many of today's leading Christians sat, in childhood, through what they recall as 'the stifling boredom of the organized church'. But ground was ploughed, into which spiritual seed was sown, which has now borne fruit for which we today are profoundly grateful. (How many were turned away is unrecorded.)

If children are needing a church life geared to their needs, then perhaps this is the time for their parents to relinquish their much-loved denominational ties? If the church of their denomination is not at all child-orientated, then perhaps, like some other families, they should seek another church which is both doctrinally acceptable to them, and the one in their area most adapted to meeting the needs of children.

Parents must be clear what they are seeking to provide for their children : they may want a church which will instil into the children the wealth of the traditional beliefs and practices of the denomination; they may want a church which will introduce their children in terms which a child can grasp to a God who is real and living : they will be fortunate to discover the 'ideal' church which combines both, and will probably have to face compromise somewhere.

Don and Meg are also, perhaps, in need of much thicker skins. They may need to learn to sit through a church service, ignoring what they imagine must be criticism of their wriggling offspring. This criticism may exist nowhere other than in their own fertile imaginations.

Had they had the courage to go on sitting through the services despite their discomfort, one day they might have heard words that it had never occurred to anyone else to say before (it seemed too obvious to onlookers), 'We love to see you as a family in church. It's such an encouragement. Your children make us think of Jesus and his love for children. . . .'

Or the even greater encouragement, 'We've watched you taking your children to church week after week. If you can do it, then perhaps we dare try too. . . .'

They might not ever have thought that their children could be of positive encouragement to other churchgoers : perhaps they had been unnecessarily sensitive, or too introspective? Or, perhaps, they were right, and they

83

and their fidgeting children *were* unwelcomed in that church?

They felt that as Christian parents they were failures. They had failed in two areas in which they thought Christian couples should excel : in 'family prayers' and in church attendance.

It never occurred to them that *the church* could rethink its approach, and make efforts to try to relate the *human family* to the *family of God*. They had no concept of the difference that this could make to them. It did not occur to them that a family really could worship as a family : the situation seemed hopeless and baffling.

They grew hardened to the criticism they faced from some Christian friends. They almost became immune to remarks overheard, such as, 'Don and Meg are right away from the Lord at present....'

They clung on to the fact that *God* knew their situation, and that He continued to love and care for them. They wished their position could be changed but themselves saw no solution.

As long as they were 'only two', they found few problems in relating their faith in God to everyday life and church attendance. Once they 'were three' they found unexpected, seemingly insoluble problems.

Perhaps they needed to adopt a more positive approach. They had a problem. They were not the first to encounter such a problem. So, they would not allow it to defeat them. They would fight to the end, for the sake of their children, to sort out these problems. If helpful they would thrash out these problems with other Christian families, and try to help one another; they would talk to their minister, and see if he could help.

One fact was certain (on which a whole book could be written) : their children needed the church, and the church needed their children. They would do their utmost to see that the two met.

11. When it Goes Wrong

Facts force us to admit that marriages between Christians do sometimes go wrong. More go wrong than many of us tend to realize. While the majority of couples manage to sort out their problems, and stay together in a growing and deepening relationship, some find that they are unable to do so. Words cannot describe the 'hell on earth' of a breaking, or destroyed, marriage. Pain and deep emotional hurt cannot be easily shared or understood by those who have never experienced it.

After nearly five years of marriage, Pam decided she must leave Mike, for the sake of her children. He was hitting her in front of them frequently, and she felt that they were growing so increasingly insecure that she must act responsibly and move them into a more stable environment. She walked out of home one day, and for her children's sake, now feels unable to return. She doubts if Mike wants her and the children back anyway.

'What about your church?' I asked her.

'They've been marvellous,' she quickly replied. 'I might have been afraid to leave Mike, because of their criticism, but the state of the children *forced* me to leave. To my surprise everyone was very kind. I didn't feel they rebuked me for what I'd done : and at first they didn't know *why* we'd separated. . . .' I sat listening as she continued, 'The only trouble was that I had hardly left Mike before they were talking about *divorce*. I wasn't even sure whether I wanted a divorce at that point; I was numb and unable to think clearly. They kept on saying that I could divorce him, but could only remarry if he had committed adultery. . . .'

'If you were divorced, might you re-marry?' I presumed to ask.

She nodded frankly, 'If the right man came along, I think I might. I can't believe that God, who is so loving, doesn't understand my situation, and care for my children – He knows how much difference a truly loving human father would make to my children's development and stability. I know some Christians feel I should never re-marry. . . .'

Pam has faced the reality of marriage breakdown, and as a Christian decided she had to leave her husband. Her church, well known for its faithful Bible teaching, has not condemned her. Behind these simple sentences lie years of agonizing heart-searching, and suffering, by this Christian couple. Marriage was 'hell on earth' for them, even though they were both Christians.

What about the Christian couple whose marriage is just beginning to go wrong? Usually their viciously descending spiral of frustration and despair is hidden under masks of normality. The mental anguish is unrecorded and unmeasurable. Does one partner run straight home to Mum? Do they pack it in quickly and quietly? Do they carry on 'business as usual' and pretend that there is no festering sore hidden under the surface of their marriage?

Most Christian couples tend to respond, 'We vowed we would stick by one another till we were parted by death . . . somehow we must make "a go" of this.' The community which witnessed their public commitment encourages them to try and stay together.

A superficial response may be glibly to say, 'We'll pray about it!' Then to assume that everything *must* be all right again.

Prayer is assumed to be a magical formula that will automatically right that which is wrong. Prayer for help in trouble is a natural and right response. The Christian passing through such deep waters should cry to his heavenly Father for help in this as in all situations : if he does not, he may need to take stock of his Christianity again. A prayer for help is not the *only* step to be taken.

Many couples need to take a harder step than this. Many need to admit to *themselves* as individuals (before they can admit to God and their marriage partner) that something has gone wrong. Some find it easier to live a lie than to admit such painful truth, even to themselves.

It's easier to live in the 'Never Never land' of marriage, as the T.V. adverts depict it, than to admit to the truth.

The courage that faces the truth, does not flee from hurtful reality; it turns in prayer to the God who created marriage, 'God, you know what's wrong, please help us out of this mess.'

Having admitted reality to oneself and to God, it may still be hard for certain Christians to face the truth with their marriage partner. It is easier to shut the truth within oneself than bring the trouble out into the open.

'After all,' they may unconsciously reason, 'as a Christian I'm supposed to "have victory" in all areas of my life . . . failure in marriage might be equated with failure as a Christian . . . I don't want to be thought to be a second-class Christian. . . .'

In no area of life can reality be escaped : it must be faced. How can we, as Christians, live a lie, and still follow him who is the truth?

Somehow, a couple must be able to talk about how and why things have gone wrong. Honesty and frankness are needed; without bitterness or accusation. How easy to write : yet, how hard to practise! Stalemate will continue until the couple really communicate and get down to the nitty-gritty of what is wrong. How tragic that Christian couples can exist in a state of stagnant non-communication. They may even 'pray' together daily (to him who is the truth) to keep alive the pretence of a happy marriage, to try to hide the truth from themselves and others.

All kinds of problems may be discovered when the couple begin to communicate : problems over money; disciplining children; getting on with in-laws; use of recreation time, etc. The fact that the couple are at odds, and are not one socially, mentally, or spiritually often means that sexual union has been neglected. This is only a symptom of underlying trouble.

However, a marriage is not necessarily 'on the rocks' because one partner feels unwilling or unable to participate in sexual intercourse. Physical or mental illness, or nothing more than tiredness, may lead to this. If a couple are able to talk about this, then understanding will enable one not to feel unwanted or rejected.

Couples need to understand their partner's reactions to stress situations, and realize how these affect their sexual feelings. When a man feels his security is threatened in any way, he may experience a deep need for the support of his wife, expressed through sexual union. Major crises, trouble at work, etc., may lead him to long for and have a deep need of sexual intercourse. On the other hand, his wife tends to react to stress by wanting to curl up, go to sleep, and have nothing to do with love-making until her situation is secure again. She would appreciate it more if her husband expressed his love by washing-up the supper dishes; feeding and bathing the baby; and giving her an evening 'off' from domestic duties.

Any married couple must learn to express their sexual feelings to one another, so that the differences in their make-up can be understood and compensated for by their partner. A man who has been led to believe a popular saying that 'an orgasm a day keeps boredom away', may be relieved to discover that his wife is quite likely to hold a different view. He may be *relieved* to find that he does not *have* to live up to someone else's standard to try and please his wife (or to prove his masculinity to himself).

Communication about the root causes of anger may be vital if a couple are to live together. The wife, whose husband walks in through the door, and starts a row about 'nothing' may, after a few weeks, want to leave him. If she probes deeply into his feelings and thoughts, she may discover that his anger arises from a sense of injustice at the way he is being treated at work. She should feel *complimented*! He is unconsciously trusting her enough to express his deepest feelings by being cross with her. If she understands this, she is more likely to stick to him, than to leave him. Such understanding comes only as a couple communicate with one another at deep levels.

As a couple begin to share the *real* reasons why they find one another hard to live with, they may feel hurt, resentful, and misunderstood. If a Christian couple are realistically going to *work* to save their marriage, then they must learn to freely forgive and accept one another as they are.

Forgiveness must be free, and be given with no strings attached. 'I'll forgive you, if you promise not to do it again!' is *not* enough.

We are to 'forgive as we are forgiven', Jesus tells us.

God forgives completely, even when He knows we will repeat our dismal failure. Our pattern for forgiveness and acceptance of fellow-men and our marriage partners, is to be that which God shows us. We must learn to forgive ourselves, and start again with the 'clean slate' which God has already given us with His forgiveness.

This all sounds so easy. Too easy to be true for many !

Some Christian couples *will* say that this works in practice, and that they have emerged with their marriages intact and enriched. However, some others will confess that it has not been easy, nor has it 'worked' for them.

The wife who woke up one day, looked at her husband and thought, 'I can and do no longer love him !', may never have found any solution as to how she can go on living with this man. There is *nothing* left between them. What does she do? There is no glib, trite, easy 'Christian solution' to her problem.

Others face problems that they are *unable* to sort out on their own. They need courage to seek the help of others. They may need courage because, for some Christians, to admit to failure in marriage is to fear that they will immediately lose their valued 'success motif' in their Christian group. They will be known for what they really are (as they see it, 'failures'). They may feel their confidences will spread around : and what is told in private may become public. I see those with the 'success motif' so valued by Christians as those who are honest enough to face reality. I see no 'success motif' attached to the hypocrisy of pretending to be what one is not.

Couples courageous enough to seek help may be fortunate enough to find a Christian couple who are able to help them. They may be able to turn to the minister of their church. Perhaps the future will bring Christian counselling centres to which they can turn. If there is no help available from specifically Christian sources, then they may feel they should seek professional help from a marriage guidance counsellor. Some Christians have found help from the Marriage Guidance Council, and no attempt has been made to alter their Christian faith.

Since Christians vow to the God they serve that they will stay with their marriage partner all their lives, surely they must make every effort to fulfil their promise? This may involve painful admission of truth, and the removal of hypocritical masks. It may involve admission to a Christian sub-culture that they have not met the standards they feel this demands of them. They may fear rejection by their sub-culture, and that they have failed.

If, however, all the pain of facing reality ultimately leads to the re-establishment of life's most precious human relationship, then surely it is worth while. The God who created the marriage relationship lovingly accepts and encourages those who feel cast out by their Christian group.

Man may reject but God accepts. He, who suffered terribly at the hands of men, understands how much we hurt one another. He knows the 'hell on earth' an unhappy marriage can bring. He promises comfort to the 'brokenhearted', and incredibly that 'all things will work together for good' to those who love Him.

12. Happily Ever After

As she passed me a cup of coffee, I noticed, for the first time, her engagement ring.

'She's getting married next April,' Michael commented.

I nodded, vaguely, not very interested as I barely knew her.

'She's read what you've written so far about marriage . . .' he continued.

I sat up. I *was* interested now.

'What does she think?' I asked : not anticipating the reply.

He knew me well enough to come straight to the point. 'She says, "Is it really as bad as that?"'

My heart sank.

What had I said to make her react in this way, I wondered? I re-read the material, I had been trying to be objective, realistic, and not to 'spiritualize-away' problems in marriage. I *had* made it sound difficult.

Since no two marriages are alike, perhaps none of the problems about which I had written would ever occur in her life. Since no prototype for the ideal Christian marriage exists, it is impossible to write a book portraying exactly the kind of marriage which two Christians must strive for. People are different, and therefore their relationships within marriage will differ. There is no such thing as 'the ideal Christian marriage pattern'.

On the back cover of her book, *The Adventure of Being a Wife*, Mrs. Norman Vincent Peale is quoted as saying, 'I consider myself one of the most fortunate women alive.

'Why?

'Because I am totally married to a man in every sense of the word : physically : emotionally : intellectually : spiritually. . . . This is such a marvellous and joyous thing that nothing else in my life can approach it. It is the greatest of all adventures.'

She's a *woman* who derives deep satisfaction in being a wife. Marriage for her was a *wonderful* adventure. I will let a *man*, who has a totally different, but equally satisfying, marriage have the final word. Having met both him and his wife briefly, I could not resist writing to ask him how his marriage worked out in practice. He is a busy, respected and fulfilled clergyman. He replied,

'You ask for a *personal* account. My "allowing" my wife to develop as a person (even the way we express it is grotesque!) was based on two convictions. Firstly there was the sheer illogicality of one partner enjoying a much wider professional and social freedom than the other. Secondly, was the recognition that my *own* wife has a range of human and personal gifts which range far beyond the kitchen sink (and considerably overshadow my own gifts in some areas!).

'These current convictions were really only fully formulated after the event. The precipitating factor in our own relationship was a depressive period for my wife after a miscarriage, which called for a practical adjustment in our roles as parents, and in our relationships with others.'

I had presumed to ask how they overcame the risk of 'competing' with one another. He replied,

'Of course there is a competitive element in any attempt at dual-career living – sometimes we both have arranged committees or interviews for the same time, when one of us has to be child-minding. But this does not invalidate it as a life-style. Sometimes I feel frustrated and irritated at having to alter my arrangements and secretly feel it would be good to have a domesticated wife who made no such out-of-home demands. But a moment's reflection reminds me that such an "ideal" is an unreal myth in any relationship, and if it were realized, the frustration of living with such a boring domesticated creature would be worse!'

Of course I wanted to know what he made of Paul's teaching about husbands being the 'head' of the wife. He continues,

'On the "head" of the wife question, I don't think I have a definitive answer. But I suspect that a lot hangs on our confusion between "authority" and "authoritarian" which is further confounded by a post-industrialization perspective (the family as a unit of consumption with the male as the chief breadwinner).

'I have never been able to take seriously the "Who decides what?" question. I would hope that if a marriage had any Christian integrity whatsoever, the answer would be "we both decide". I cannot see otherwise how Christians can read verses about mutual sharing, fellowship, and having a common mind. But then I suppose the question becomes: what if each holds a firm opposite opinion? I cannot recall where this has actually happened in any important situation in our marriage. I think this is because one of us will give way to the other whose interests we feel to be more at stake (or whose opinions are more to be valued on that subject). For example, if I was really keen on a job, I don't think my wife would stand in my way, without having very good grounds for querying the situation.

'A more recent example would be my wife having invited a twenty-year-old girl into our home for several weeks. The situation with this particular girl I find objectively difficult; but I would not stand in the way of my wife exercising this law of minority (unless it produced a very high level of domestic strain!).

'This, I think, also answers your question about avoiding being a "doormat". We avoid this by a system of mutual compromise, and give-and-take in successive situations, to prevent either of us becoming a doormat. From time to time, one of us may feel ill-treated. I find it personally threatening when my wife has a very quick succession of professional engagements, Christian committees, counselling sessions in the home with people in need, so that we scarcely converse for several days (i.e. we rarely meet!). But then I am likely to express my feelings as we seek to work towards a more balanced situation.

' "Who does the housework?" you ask.

'The frank answer to that one is mostly no one! This seems an inevitable consequence of spreading one's interests in other directions; I don't see how being intensely house-proud can co-exist with a dual-career family (unless you pay someone to do the housework). The more practical answer is that we *both* do routine housework. I seldom cook, but I usually wash up, and often make the beds. I think we are helped by clashing temperaments at this point. I find it difficult to live for a long period with books out of place and cluttered tables, but a bit of dust does not bother me. My wife finally gets ashamed of dust on furniture and floors but is maddeningly indifferent to general clutters. So it works quite well.

'My wife certainly does not work because we need the money, in the sense that a woman might go reluctantly to work but would rather be at home. Of course the supplemented income is pleasant (one might almost say imperative for clergy) but the real reason she works is for her own fulfilment as a person. In Christian circles there is often an atmosphere of disapproval that wives should seek such fulfilment. Such pressure seems to me to be immoral in so far as it can give rise to unnecessary guilt feelings. Moreover it is entirely without biblical foundation (which relates to the necessary care of children by the wife, and not to the exclusion of other work and interests).

'You ask whether I would rather have a wife free from other work worries to be concerned about mine. I'm sure I don't desire anything quite as simple as that. I am not a great advocate of the image of the clergy-wife as an unpaid parish worker, although it would be undesirable if she were not willing to support her husband's role to the extent of a reasonable amount of entertaining, etc. My own personal experience of clergy families (where the wife is freed to "worry about her husband's parish problems") is that the freedom is an acute form of bondage, sometimes producing boring and rather colourless individuals.

'The *real* tension, from my point of view, is in the balance between our respective professional roles in out-of-work time (i.e. entertaining, and evening committees, etc.) all of which can eat up relaxation time, and time given to family interests. I find that a spate of concentrated busyness of this kind begins to knot me up in an unhelpful way. But I do not think this is a valid argument against the well-planned dual-career situation (which we achieve most of the time). Moreover it is very much a question of temperament. There are many clergy who seem to thrive on continuous activism, whereas I begin to shrivel if I do not get time for quiet reading, etc.

'My basic position is that I am suspicious of generalizations on marriage patterns, and especially evangelical Christian generalizations, except in so far as they refer to the wider qualities of all Christian living (practical love, mutual understanding and sharing, patience, the value of each individual, and so on). Christians are generally bad sociologists and frequently invest with authority some cultural tradition. I am not as impressed by the quality of the middle-class Victorian family as some people.'

No two marriages will ever be the same! If we feel like staggering under the weight of the realization that to marry is not automatically to 'live happily ever after', we may need to dump our heavy load on the floor.

We must realize that a happy marriage entails *work* : not tottering around, moaning that the load is too great, and we are too weak and human to carry it. Therefore, we will moan and not even try our hardest!

The load must be left on the floor, and not be allowed to crush us. We must learn to shift the load into God's hands and to apply God's promises to our marriages. He says, 'My grace is sufficient for you, for my power is made perfect in weakness.'

God's power can transform our lives, and our marriages. In Him we find the courage both to marry and to stay married.

Humanly speaking we cannot : but with God, we have the courage to try.

'Dare you . . .?' My children's voices as they play float up from the garden as I write.

I mentally reply, 'I *dare* . . . but I only have the courage to dare because God promises to go all the way with me . . . I daren't on my own.'

Anne Townsend Titles

PRAYER WITHOUT PRETENDING

Can praying for other people be reduced to a
mathematical equation? Does an omnipotent God need
our prayers? What place does prayer have in an age of
instant everything? Or is it just a lazy way of helping?
Or is prayer only for the un-young, un-contemporary?

The author shares frankly with readers how she, as a
missionary, struggled with and resolved her doubts and
questionings about intercessory prayer.

FAMILIES WITHOUT PRETENDING

Families are under attack.

Why live in families anyway? Is the traditional family
unit of one dad, one mum and their kids really a good
thing? Why not a commune, or some other alternative?

And how? How to live in families? If you survive the
early years, 'teenagers can be time-bombs'. Honest
Christian parents would admit that their faith grants
them far from total immunity from family problems.

Anne Townsend, who is a doctor, and mother of three,
writes about both the 'why' and the 'how' questions of
living in families. She has a gift for relating Biblical
principles to contemporary experiences.